DOORWAY TO SPIRIT

By Devin Listrom

Doorway to Spirit

By Devin Listrom
Illustrations by Adam Tillery and Kristina McPheeters
Photos by Devin Listrom and Margie Kay
Copy Editor: Judith Listrom
Editor: Margie Kay

Copyright © 2020 by Devin Listrom

Cover art: Adobe Stock Ogrodowa brama z bluszczem nocą
By Unholy Vault Designs

First Printing: 2020

ISBN: 978-0-9988558-7-5

Un-X Media Publishing
PO Box 1166
Independence, MO 64050
www.unxmedia.com
816-833-1602

Ordering Information: Special discounts are available on quantity purchases by corporations, associations, educators, and others. For details, contact the publisher at the above listed address.

UNXMEDIA

PUBLISHING

CONTENTS

Acknowledgements v

Introduction 7

Chapter 1 The Period 13

Chapter 2 Psychic Realms 25

Chapter 3 Family Experiences – Grandpa
Cookie 37

Chapter 4 Journeys to Colorado 53

Chapter 5 Spirit Vision 63

Chapter 6 Group Investigations 91

Chapter 7 Awareness 115

Chapter 8 Solitary Investigations 155

Conclusion 173

About the Author 175

Publications by Un-X Media 176

Acknowledgements

I would like to thank my teachers, my editor, and my family without whose help this book would never have been completed.

Thank you for your patience and guidance, and your use of the editor's red pen...

Introduction

It has been a long journey writing this book, and an even longer journey going through the experiences leading to this book. I am excited to be sharing this story with readers. This writing is not to change anyone's beliefs, but to take the reader through my personal experiences with spirits and dealings of the paranormal as if the reader were walking through a museum and I am the tour guide.

Before I started on this project, I had no idea I would be turning it into a book. In my late 30's I kept saying to myself "I need to document all of these experiences." When I hit forty years of age, I began to ask myself some profoundly serious questions. I spent years working jobs I was not always happy with, and it was the same thing with freelance jobs. The big question was "What is my purpose in life?" I began to hit rock bottom at this time and suffered serious depression for several months. It really terrified me. I thought I was not going to survive the depression. But it finally passed.

I took an acting job at one of the haunted houses during October 2011. It was fun most of the time. We all had to be there a couple of hours before the doors opened. It seemed I was the easiest actor to scare in the house by other actors. They even gave me an award for it. They also had Elvira Mistress of the Dark there one night. And I got my picture taken with her, which is still have in my possession. While waiting to be let in, I would always go out to my car and listen to Opera and write in my diary about all my paranormal experiences. As I began to write I still had no idea that I would eventually turn it into a book for the world to read. I got to a point and it seemed I was being guided. The writing was taking on a noticeable new form. I decided to read back through the material. A huge vision came to me saying to share your stories with humanity. I also felt the spirits wanted their stories told.

This new goal/purpose is to become a writer of the paranormal. Another part of the goal is to help people with their homes and business with spirit activity. Also, to work as a Reiki Energetic healer for people and animals and offer psychic readings for those who seek spiritual messages. I also have a huge interest in working on missing persons cases utilizing my psychic abilities. People are missing every day.

I will be talking about real investigations and psychic work communicating with spirits in this book. These occurrences began when I was five years of age. I began to hear spirit voices and seeing a black apparition at that time. At age six dead people started coming to me and I had no idea why. At this age, a kid most likely has no understanding of death.

I eventually became interested in Halloween. Every year I was watching the calendar for the next Halloween. Collecting fake skulls and scary music soundtracks. Dracula was a big draw for me and dressing up in costumes. I never really got into anything grotesque. Later I learned the ancient roots to Halloween come from the Celtic People. They called it "Samhain" (pronounced so-wain). Which is based on a Sabbat celebration of our ancestors and their memory. And still being celebrated today.

School was a troubling time for me. I was always tense in the classroom. There were kids in the neighborhood that I kept getting into trouble with, but once they all moved away my life became noticeably quiet. I got along better with adults than other kids my age. When I turned sixteen, I volunteered at an event called "Terror Train." It was a fundraiser for the Kansas City zoo. I played different characters like Norman Bates, a graveyard ghost, and one of the chainsaw massacres. This event closed and I ended up working at the haunted house in the downtown area. This time I got paid to scare people.

A main part of my goal is not to just prove the existence of spirits but the fact they can communicate with us. Many people have been reporting experiences with spirits and ghosts for centuries. I am not sure how it can be debunked when these continued reports go on being reported. Various types of evidence have been brought forward over the years. Since photography began, spirits or some type of apparition has often been captured on film and voice recorders have also caught voices or footsteps. Spirit orbs are the most common things caught in photos and on video.

One early technique was used to spread white powder on the floor and wait to see if any hand or footprints showed up in the powder. Spirit boards, dowsing rods and more modern equipment have been invented to enhance communication with spirits such as EVP (Voice recorders) EMF detectors and thermo cams. This type of electronic equipment keeps advancing. Now we have reality television shows about various groups who investigate these paranormal claims, from ghosts to UFO activity. It really shows how humanity seeks to know if there is an afterlife. I believe there is an afterlife. Looking at the Celts and the Egyptians, they had a strong belief in the afterlife. They even would bury their dead with their finest clothing and materials to prepare them for the afterlife.

Another part of my goal is to help those who feel alone. It is hard to share paranormal and psychic experiences. People are fast to judge you as if you were crazy, but you are not. Believing in your spiritual experiences is no different than those who believe in God.

Over the years as I would build my psychic abilities and experiences with paranormal investigations it came to my attention that there are a lot of investigators who have a passion for this type of work. And there are those who are not serious about it and go as thrill seekers. I do not believe this is helping spirits or clients. It is very irresponsible. We all need to take care on investigations. Situations which involve entering abandoned buildings or houses is not a good idea. There is the legal matter of entering abandoned locations, not to mention physical safety. Signs saying "KEEP OUT" are there for a reason. Plus, unknown entities could follow people home if they do not know how to protect themselves.

Another matter I have experienced with other investigators is skepticism towards psychics. I believe these people need to learn how to tune in to their abilities, because I think we all have psychic abilities. I usually like to do the psychic work at the first part of an investigation in order to get the spirits to tell me their story about why they are there. Sometimes I get visions of spirits or an actual scene, or I feel their emotions of fear or depression empathically. I also psychically hear spirits talk, which is known as clairaudience. Meditation always helps me to center and protect myself while working on cases. Centering is when I balance my energies with energies of earth and heaven. Then I build a protective light around myself. But it also allows me to open myself up to the spirit world to begin communication.

Technical equipment such as EVP recorders or digital photos can be matched with psychic findings. I put myself in a state called "Alpha State" prior to an investigation. Alpha is where I do my best work. I began to explore with this idea. Then with practice, I figured out that by quieting my mind I quiet the conscious mind. Then I realized my subconscious mind really came alive. Being amazed at this outcome, I then realized my psychic abilities come from the subconscious mind. The more I practiced the shaper my abilities became. I would call this shifting the consciousness from everyday mundane thoughts to the world of spirit. The mundane and spirit can work together, and this is what my goal is when I investigate.

I hope the reader enjoys this book.

Chapter 1

The Period

All my life I have had this lucid memory of being in the womb. This memory was in complete darkness, then moving into its opposite, the light. I remember seeing the hospital lights over me and the fact I was not crying. Everything felt subtle and quiet. My lungs were not completely developed because I was induced about three weeks early. A nurse noticed I was not breathing correctly. She got a doctor who knew how to take care of me. He put me in an incubator for about ten days. I was under weight and had a fifty percent chance of surviving. This near-death experience, I believe is when I received my gift to communicate with the spirit world.

When I was a small child, I started to have episodes of hearing voices through the wall of my bedroom. These voices would wake me up in the middle of the night. I do not remember what they were saying but I remember hearing actual voices. They sounded blurred and with a low pitch. I think it was two spirits talking to me or about me. I had no understanding what was happening at the time. They could have been spirit guides of mine. My sister eventually took the middle bedroom next to my parent's room on the opposite side of the hallway. This made me become isolated from everyone in the house. This is when I believe the spirits began working on me.

It was not just the voices I heard. I had my first occurrence with a full apparition when I was about five years old. I saw this black figure appearing to be human walking by my bedroom window. At least I thought it was something human. It passed my bedroom every night for several months. I could not hear any footsteps or any kind or sound of someone moving around outside. But I knew someone, or something, was out there. The more it made its presence known to me in the window, the more I feared this entity.

This fear magnified when I was awakened during a rainstorm late one night. I felt I was being pulled out of a deep sleep and I noticed my bedroom door was open. When I could hear the rain hitting the house with a huge force, I knew something was getting ready to happen. When I looked up, I saw a tall black figure in the shape of a human standing in my bedroom doorway. It was faceless and the top of the head was flat. Then a sudden feeling I had was total terror and I pulled the covers over my head. It had to be the same black figure from the window.

This entity came into our house and revealed itself to me directly. I felt as though it was saying to me "I am here". What was this entity thinking? What was it going to do? I do not think it was a human spirit, but rather an unknown entity. I could not tell if it was going to do harm to me, but it was sure giving me a good scare. I never told my parents or anyone else about it. I kept these experiences to myself for a long time.

The entity was not yet finished with me. I had a dream where my family and I were in the living room. The front door was wide open. Fog began to surround the house and it was extremely thick, and it was completely dark outside. In the fog we could see only one streetlight was working. It seemed the entire street was filled with fog. Then we all were startled at the black faceless figure slowly coming out of the fog. It looked right at us making its way to the house.

My dad had one foot outside the front door and pointed at it and yelled out "There it is! It's coming towards us!" He pulled us into a circle and told us to make a run for it. The faceless black figure quickly disappeared. I suddenly woke up on the living room floor in the dark. I was evidently in a deep sleep the entire time, though I knew I started out in bed before the dream. Did this entity cause me to sleepwalk? After the dream, the entity never showed itself to me again. Was I being tested? Perhaps the entity had completed its purpose by letting me know I could see what other people could not.

Early Experiences - Phil

During these early years of my life many family members and pets made their presence known to me after death. I saw my step-grandfather, Phil, who died in 1976 from an aortic aneurysm. He was married to my paternal grand-mother, Mary Liz. They had a good marriage for about two years. Being a wood carver, he had carved me a Christmas necklace that represented an Egyptian goddess named Isis when I was age seven. It was based off a television show in the 1970's. It was my favorite present.

However, my step-grandfather had a history of alcoholism. He was sober during their marriage because my grand-mother would not put up with it. The doctor told him he would die if he ever drank again. After two years he had an alcoholic meltdown, and it took his life. Towards the end my grandmother asked him why he did it. He said he would tell her when he came home. He never made it home. He died suddenly and took his secret to his grave.

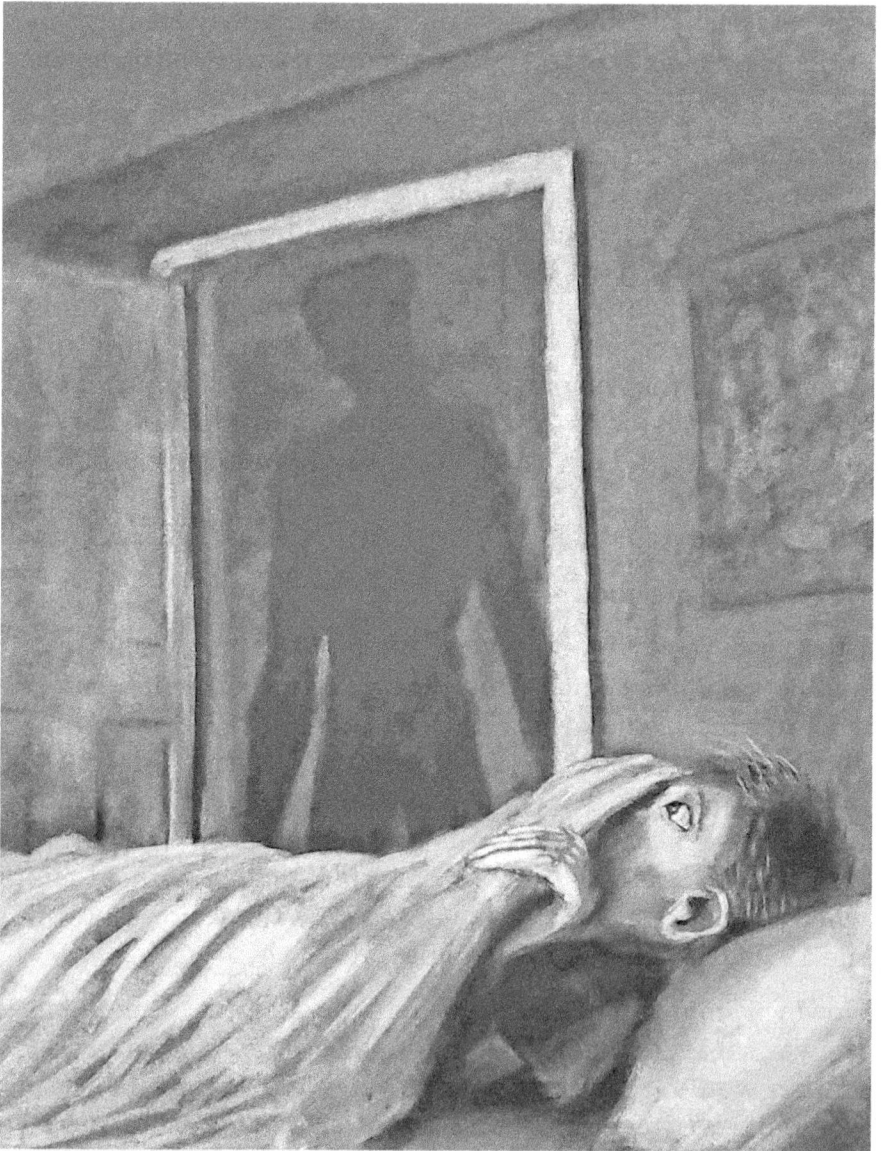

Figure 1 Flathead guy   illustration by Adam Tillery

When he passed, I remember going to the funeral in Parkville. I remember asking my mother "Are we going to see him in the little bed?" She said, "Yes, we are going to see him in the little bed." This was a time when I was figuring out what death was. He came to me a couple of times after he died. He was appearing to me on a psychic level from the shoulders up. He was smiling at me and saying his final goodbye. I have always believed he enjoyed our company. This happened extremely fast.

Early experiences – Aunt Ruby

On the day in 1978 of my great-aunt Ruby's passing, I was visiting my grandmother, Mary Liz. Her minister came to see her and to announce Aunt Ruby had died in her house. I remember seeing Mary Liz crying over the news. When the minister left, I was thinking "Aunt Ruby is gone." She then appeared to me on several occasions in less than a week.

Ruby lived alone for quite some time in a large three level brick house. The funeral home in Parkville for the service was across the street from her house. This experience was a little scary for me. As I looked upon her in the casket it seemed she was moving. I knew she could not be moving. On every look, though, I would see her head moving side to side. As the evening progressed, I kept seeing her move her head and then her arms. This was putting my mind on a trip. I kept on telling myself she was not moving.

Later in the night as I was getting ready for bed, I felt I was not alone in my room. This feeling became a vision when my great-aunt appeared before me. I could see her from the neck up intuitively, through my third eye, not my physical eyes. Fear did come over me at first, but I do not think her intentions were to scare me. She had the look on her face she always had in her later years of life. This look was sad and lifeless. I looked up some old family photos. During the search I found a good number of photos with her sad facial expression. This was validation for me, but what was the cause? She endured a bad marriage twice with the same abusive husband and lost a child at birth. She never recovered from these experiences. For her remaining years she lived alone in a deep state of depression taking over her entire being. After she appeared to me a few times, I think she finally figured out she was dead. I never saw or felt her presence again.

Early experiences - The old brick house

This childhood experience is incredibly special to me. As a small child I was already communicating with spirits. But I was not fully aware of it, even though there were specifics. In a sense I was doing my first reading on an actual location at the age of 6 or 7. During the early fall season of 1976 or 1977 my grandfather Cookie would have me over on the weekends. Right next door to him was an old brick house and it was vacant at the time and even a little run down. When my parents would drive up to my grandfather's house, I started to get a feeling the house next door was not so vacant. But I still knew no one was living there, at least not in physical form.

Every time my parents were dropping me off, I felt a pull to go over to the old brick house and peek in the side door window. The house was emptied out and the only thing I remember seeing was an old black stove. This stove looked like it had been used a lot. It only worked with a fire.

It became a habit to run over and peek inside. on one occasion I was by the side door and I heard a loud noise, but it was subtle at the same time. this noise came from the inside

Figure 2 Grace's Kitchen Door

of the house. As if someone was moving around in there. I told my parents about the loud noise inside the old brick house. They told me that no one lives there right now. I would tell them a lady lives in that house and she made a loud sound. My mother told me to go inside with grandfather

I could not get the sound I heard and the lady inside the house next door who got my attention out of my head. This continued for weeks. I started to feel like I had to go over and peek in the side door each time. This lady spirit who I was not able to see with my physical eyesight, but only with an intuitive vision seemed to enjoy my company. I never feared her. But I would feel the curiosity and the excitement of the experience. Even today as an adult the same curiosity runs with me. Every time I would go over to the old brick house next door, I would tell my parents there is a lady in there and I would point my finger. I think they thought I was just imagining things because no one would take me seriously on the issue. I began to just keep it to myself.

One occasion when I was peeking in the side window, I sensed the same female presence and it seemed like she was doing her regular daily routine. A vision of her came to me and she was wearing a long black dress with an apron. Her hair was up in a bun and she was thinking to herself how she needed to get all her work done that day. Another part of the vision was of her taking things out of the hot oven and putting things in. It looked like she was cooking for people. Maybe some kind of business or volunteer community work, but it looked like she was preparing for an event. I also saw her working up a good sweat from an extremely hot kitchen.

When I first looked over the photos during the background research in 2018, I saw her in one being young and a second photo of her being older. This was when I remembered seeing her young in my vision, and the photo below really stood out. I picked up the photo and said to myself "this is her". It was an exciting moment.

Now in my adult years I look back at this experience and I can still feel the excitement and the curiosity. Then I started to ask myself who was the lady next door in the old brick house. I told my mother this experience for the first time in years and she was amazed I was picking up on spirits at such a young age. She did say that the lady's name was Ms. Kahm, and her first name was Grace. Her family came to Parkville MO in the month of May 1855 from Prussia. Her father was named Fritz. His wife's family name was Klamm. Other siblings were Fred, Lizzie, Minnie, and Walter.

Grace graduated from Park College in Parkville MO in 1895 cum laude, which she mentioned to people quite often at the time. She even held a graduation party at her house.

Grace was known to put on parties of different kinds. I believe it was one of her parties she was preparing for in my vision, working over a hot oven with food.

FIGURE 3 GRACE IN THE CENTER

In 1905 Grace worked for Children's Mercy Hospital for six years (1912-1918), then was working as the city collector of Parkville from (1948-1951).

A story I found about her indicated that she was not too fond of children. She had problems with them getting into her garden. It is known that two boys got into her garden and took a bunch of grapes. This became very surprising to me, since I was only seven years old, when she called me over to see what she was doing. Now I tend to ask myself, was she there for real in spirit as in conscious activity? Or did she leave part of herself behind as an energetic pattern which repeats over and over?

She spent her remaining years in the family home and died on September 6, 1963. I still do not think this an experience to be afraid of, but rather to cherish.

Early Experiences – Operation White Light

At the age of ten I was in the fourth grade. I had just started going to a different elementary school. My grandmother was a teacher there at the time and I could not get away with anything. I remember a girl in the hallway kicked me in the leg for no reason, I tried to kick her back, but my grandmother caught me.

One day I had a doctor's visit. I had a condition becoming serious which called for surgery. The doctor felt I was a little too young to be having this experience, but it was real.

The day came for the operation and was I rolled into the surgical room. I was moved onto the table and above me was a huge light. I remember the nurse telling me to take in a deep breath of something smelling sweet. The very next thing, I was getting up from the operating table as my physical body remained. As I was floating to the top of the room, I began looking down on the operating table as the doctor stood over me. I could see the surgical lights and white clothing the doctor was wearing. As this continued, I noticed a force pulling me towards an amazing bright light.

This light began to surround my entire being. It seemed to be the tunnel of the light of heaven, making me feel warm and safe. Then I heard an indescribable voice. It was saying to me I needed to turn around and go back, my purpose was not yet fulfilled. In no time at all I awakened in recovery in total agony. A nurse with this huge smile and large glasses asked me if I was okay. Then I slept for the next two to three days. I was trying to figure out what happened to the wonderful light that made me feel so good. In fact, I believe I began looking for it. I wanted to go back to this light and let it surround me again. This was an experience I will never forget.

Early Family Experiences - My Teacher

As I moved through the sixth grade, I had a good teacher-student relationship with a special reading teacher. When I got into the ninth grade my grandmother told me she was extremely sick. I believe it was some type of cancer. We both paid her a visit, and I took her some flowers and we had a nice talk. The memory I still have is of her in a body brace, from her neck down to her legs. A month later she passed on. Soon after, a vision was shown to me of her in a photo frame. This frame began to move towards me and got larger and larger. It seemed like her eyes were looking right into my eyes. I knew she was totally conscious of me. Knowing she was already dead; this experience became a little startling. I remembered she was such a nice person in life, and she would not frighten or hurt anyone for any reason. This experience happened three different times. Each time the frame got closer and closer. This could have been her way of saying goodbye.

There was a change in my life at this point. Some new kids moved into the neighborhood. This event turned out to be a huge long-term distraction from my spiritual and psychic growth. I was always getting into trouble with these kids. As it turned out, some of them were not friends, but bullies.

They kept my life in turmoil all the time. All the commotion was too much for me to take so when they all moved away a tremendous weight was lifted off my shoulders. I was around thirteen years of age. I spent the next few years as a couch potato and gained weight.

Through junior high school I was not very social and kept to myself. Then in high school I was able to lose the weight I gained. During these years, fitness became a huge focus with cardio activity and weight training. In 1986, I started to teach classes and I got into herbal remedies. My fitness years lasted for about twelve years. After high school I had a desire to become an opera singer. I started to study at the Kansas City Conservatory of Music with private teachers and majoring in voice performance. And I absolutely loved the historical music, like Mozart and Verdi. There was one scene for Don_Giovanni_where I studied the role of a retired Commander who is killed by Don Giovanni and comes back as a ghost. I discovered I was a bass-baritone. For many years I visualized myself at the MET, Royal Opera or La Scala.

Then the healing work introduced itself to me. I suddenly realized I was not supposed to be on the opera stage. All my plans were turned around without warning. The spirit world finally got me going in a new direction to continue their guidance for me to meet a teacher in the physical world.

Chapter 2

Psychic Realms

When I turned 22 years old, I met a spiritual consultant named Patricia. She was living near my parents and where I went to high school. My mom got a reading from her. She recommended that I go see her for a reading as well. Pat told me of a psychic development class she taught. This was when I started to learn about meditation. It was quite evident Pat was the teacher my spirit guides led me to. I worked with her for several years. I have remained in contact with her since then.

I met some wonderfully spiritual people at these classes. Patricia would have us do readings for each other in the class in different ways. One of the ways we did readings was by holding a personal item belonging to someone else in the class. When I picked up an item like keys or a ring, I had no idea who it belonged to. As I did these readings, I asked my spirit guides what is in the highest interest of this person. I realized I could not second guess myself and everything had to be from spirit.

On one occasion, I was in class one night and we all picked an item off the platter. As I held the item I began to pick up on the words "Let Go and Let God." A woman there said she had this affirmation on the wall in her bedroom at home in a picture frame. And she looks at it every single day for inspiration.

Patricia also taught other methods of doing readings. One was to have someone write their name or a question on paper. We practiced running the fingers across the writing, feeling the letters under the fingertips, and picking up on the other person's energy. This was when I started to get visions as part of the reading. I also learned when the soul leaves the body and returns it is called an OBE which means "Out of body experience". I believe another way to call it is "Astral Travel/Projection" or Bi-location. During these types of experiences there is a silver cord attached to our physical body and to our soul as it soars. I believe when we die this cord breaks.

The pendulum is another way of communicating with spirits by asking yes and no questions. I established a connection with a crystal pendulum and then held it pointing straight down. When I asked the pendulum to show me YES, it moved clockwise. Then it showed me NO by moving counterclockwise. I was excited about all this new information.

After these discoveries, I began to develop visualization skills when closing my eyes. This could be called "Scrying". This is when you are using your "Sight" or "Third eye vision". The purpose of Scrying is to get visions and messages. There is one important aspect to psychic abilities and visions: When using various tools, it is your mind doing the work, not the tools. I found that it does take a lot of practice.

In class, one of the meditations Pat taught us was the Chakra Meditation. Chakras are seven spinning discs along the center line of the body. Keeping them spiritually open is important for anyone's health. I remember closing my eyes and taking deep relaxing breaths. We would work on meditation quite often. Then I began to meditate on my own at home. One night, I did the meditation I learned in class twice. I was in such a deep state, I saw auras, different colors and shades, surrounding living things—me, the plants, and trees. As I was looking at my own aura I began to float to the top of the room and through the top of the house. It felt I was flying in the air out into space and yet I was still connected to my body. I saw the moon and then I saw the sun on the opposite side of the earth. I realized how beautiful the earth really is. Then when I started to move soaring toward the earth, I could feel my astral body floating. There was a feeling of total freedom. I thought I was going to fly directly into the earth. But I ended up landing or it felt somewhat of a crash. My body bounced at the same time. I opened my eyes and realized I had been out in the astral plane. I told Pat at the next class. She told me when I let go in meditation, astral travel can be part of the experience. I was unaware of the fact this was just the beginning of my experiences with the astral plane. But I will never forget this second occurrence.

Mythical Creatures

In this physical world we have many different types of creatures. I was still living at home and going to Pat's classes and furthering my knowledge. The meditations were really becoming a serious focus to communicate with my spirit guides. It is my belief that when we sleep, it is a perfect time for spirits to work with us or bring us messages. One night I was in a deep sleep and I noticed something at the foot end of my bed. I could hear and sense movement, but it was subtle. Still in a sleep state I sat up and saw this giant black snake or serpent of some kind. I became completely terrified and began swatting at it with my pillow. Each time I would try to swat it, I would miss. It was an enormously powerful creature, and I grew more terrified of it. Then I would wake up and it was gone, and I would be swatting at the air. The feeling of confusion took over my mind while trying to figure out what just happened. The next night this experience happened again. I would see this creature at the end of my bed, and I would swat at it with my pillow. But I could never hit it. It seemed to me I was fighting for my life with this creature. My mom would hear me screaming at it, and she was not able to get in because the door was locked. This went on for a long period of time night after night. Eventually I was able to see the eyes and I noticed it had not attacked me. It never did attack me. Looking back at this creature I began to wonder why it came into my presence.

Through the research I did on Mythical animals it made perfect sense. This was a time of transformation on a spiritual and emotional level. Due to my spiritual teachings with Pat, it was causing doors to open. I believe the snake is a symbol of rebirth and renew. When they shed off their old skin, they are leaving behind an old part of themselves which no longer serves. I also found they are a symbol of secrets. Well, all the knowledge and experiences I was gaining was a secret from most people. The only time I would talk about my psychic abilities was in Pat's class with other students.

I honestly believe this mythical black snake did come to me from a different realm, and not the physical. Another reason I think it came to me was to test if I could see it or not.

Spirits Touching

My experiences came to a turn. Being able to see and sense spirits is different from being touched. I never really thought a spirit could touch anyone. Well, they can. One night I was finishing up with a meditation. As I began to bring my consciousness back to my body and the room, I started to feel fingers going down my back and along my spine. This got my attention. Then I felt fingers going down my left arm. I started to look around the room and no one else was in there with me. I decided to go to sleep and lay on my stomach. Suddenly I was feeling fingers going down my chest and abdomen. This time I knew something was in the room because I thought no one could touch me on the chest and abdomen while I was lying on my stomach. I jumped out of bed and stood by the doorway and looked around the room again but still, no one was present. This was very disturbing to me and my meditations began to decrease. But this ability stayed with me regardless. I later discovered when spirits touch you, they are working on communication with us in the physical world. This also could have been another test to see if I could sense them and not just see them. I believe some spirits are guides. Even human spirits may communicate with us in a similar way. I had no idea at that time that more experiences were still coming.

As I look back at these tests, I believe the spirit world was seeing if I was worthy of these abilities and able to move forward with them.

It was quite evident I was letting fear take control of these experiences. I started to let distractions take place. Assuming it would make me feel less afraid. But later realized I was always safe. I tried blocking this ability. But it can stay with you whether you want it or not. I learned if I was having psychic experiences there was no need to feel afraid or ashamed. Accepting my abilities with confidence became particularly important, especially since many children and teenagers who have psychic abilities are often encouraged to stifle these abilities.

As I continued learning about my psychic abilities, I found that when a spirit was making itself known I was asking

"What can I do for you?" Some spirits like communicating and some do not. Depending on the response of the spirit or entity, I can tell if it is okay to communicate. If there is no response this could indicate the spirit may not be in my highest good.

I never had the opportunity to know other kids who were gifted with psychic abilities. If there were, they certainly were not talking. Maybe they were afraid to say anything. One thing I have learned when it comes to skeptics is, they fear what they do not understand. Some people say they need to physically see and touch to believe something is there. Well, the spirit world is very real.

The Entity in the basement PK

During the first year I was studying with Pat, I noticed a slight disturbance in our house. I did not put a lot of thought into it at first. This was during late fall or early winter in 1992-93. Walking through the hallway to my room I had to pass by the basement stairs. I kept on picking up on this disturbance with a sense of fear. One day I told my mother about this and she said she noticed it as well. Neither one of us knew what was causing it, but we both felt this sense of fear. This was a time when my dad was occupying the basement bedroom. He spent years as a child being abused by his father and dealing with bad employers as an adult. This caused him a lot of anxiety and long-term trauma.

As the weeks passed, my dad was still occupying the basement bedroom and his anxiety continued. Then he decided to stay at a place for help. The day after he left, I felt this fear increase. I began to feel scared in our own house and so did my mother. One day, I was walking to my room and passing by the basement stairs. It seemed like someone was moving around down there. The garage door and back door were both locked. I knew no one else could have been in the house. This went on for a day or two.

There were times I would dread going downstairs to do laundry. I would walk down the stairs and pass my dad's bedroom. He usually kept the door shut. Then I would walk through two connecting doors to the washing machine. Each time I had to attend to the laundry I could sense movement and feeling extreme levels of fear. Then, I had to go back up the stairs. Each time it seemed someone was right behind me. I made a habit of running back through the basement and up the stairs. No matter how fast I ran this thing ran behind me. And slammed the door shut to the basement.

One night I was in the living room, getting ready to go into my bedroom. This sense of fear was amplifying. Then I felt someone, or something was on the staircase. Then the next day this energy was at the top of the stairs. It fully acknowledged me, and I completely froze. A vision of a black entity with red eyes was staring me down.

The form of this entity looked like a black cloud. And in this black cloud I could see the lining of a human head. There were not a lot of facial features, mainly the red eyes looking at me. This happened at least two times. It was extremely terrifying.

Once I got a hold of myself, I questioned why is this entity in our house? What does it want? Eventually I figured it had to be connected to my dad in the basement bedroom. I am not sure how, but I just knew.

My mother and I continued noticing this black entity on the basement stairs, and had a great fear of it. Over the next few weeks, it began to wane. It was keeping itself in the downstairs bedroom. The longer my dad was out of the house, the weaker it became. Then we both felt a relief, it was gone. There was no sense of it, no more fear. In the year 2018 we began to talk about it again. I asked her if my dad ever talked about it with her. She said yes, he did talk to her about it at the time it was occurring.

The details were more terrifying than I thought. He told my mother this black figure would make itself known to him in the middle of the night. He would have nightmares about this thing, and he would wake up with its red eyes staring at him and would sometimes find himself cowering in a corner of the room. There were other times it would sit on the bed with him. He could feel a downward pressure on the bed, like a person was really sitting there. The house was becoming very unsettled with this entity.

One day, my mother found a place for my father to stay where he could get help for his anxiety and depression. He stayed at this place for quite a while. I remember the family went out to see him and see a group therapy session. My dad was a child of an alcoholic and many of the others were as well. He seemed to be improving as the weeks passed. When he returned home, the entity was gone. He got a new job as an accountant. This kept his mind occupied for the next ten years, and we were no longer bothered by the entity.

Window watcher

It was July 4th, 2015 and everyone was having a good time. Fireworks were going off and the weather was warm and sunny. My parents and I were watching a musical that afternoon. We had some neighbors move in across the street in a rental house a few weeks prior. This house has been known to sit empty quite often. On this festive day, these neighbors were playing music outside. An elderly neighbor living next door to my parents was feeling bothered by the music.

He was over eighty years old and served in the Korean War. He walked across the street with his cane and asked them to turn the music down. They did not want to turn the music down and it became a very heated argument. Our elderly neighbor took his cane and wacked their car with it. These neighbors called the police and one of them said "I will take care of him". After this event it seemed our elderly neighbor became very paranoid and one day he suddenly disappeared.

We thought he just was too scared to come out of his house. He would not even go over to my parent's house. There was no answer at his door or on his phone. A few nights later I was getting ready for bed. I have a staircase behind my building with a small balcony. My window faces this staircase. As I was turning out the light and getting into bed, I began to feel watched. I knew there was someone watching me from outside. Pulling over the blankets and looking out the window I saw a figure wearing rugged pants and a dark jacket, his face covered. Within a moment I began to recognize this individual. It was my parent's elderly neighbor watching in the window. Then he suddenly vanished. I began to feel a little startled and could not get to sleep.

This was on a Wednesday night, just a few days after the July 4th incident. I called my mother and told her what I witnessed, and I felt it was their elderly neighbor. She said he was nowhere to be found. Suspicion began to fill my mind on what I witnessed. Friday night was approaching, and I was going into bed. By this time, I was beginning to forget the occurrence. Then suddenly, the figure was there again on the back balcony watching me in the window. I knew who it was this time and I began to ask, "why are you on the balcony?"

This time he appeared for almost a minute. A chill ran up my spine and I had trouble sleeping again.

I told my family about this figure for the second time. I became very sure it was our elderly neighbor. They told me he has not been seen for a full week. Now it had become a missing person's case. The police came and searched the house and then the area. They found nothing. After he appeared the two times in the window, I began to place my hands over my heart. At this point I began to pick up on the possibility he was having heart troubles with a high level of fear. Had he made himself into a prisoner in his own home?

A couple of days later, on a Sunday, I was facing the bathroom mirror. The feeling of being watched began to increase. I could feel a presence of someone taller than myself standing behind me. This experience felt cold and then I became annoyed. I figured out it was the same figure from the window, our elderly neighbor. He was leaning over me and I told him he could not do that. I am willing to talk but I do not like him hovering over me. It seemed he did not like me saying that and his presence was gone. My home became noticeably quiet.

A day or two later my mom wanted to see if I could pick up on him by touching his house. I was somewhat reluctant to do that because other neighbors could be watching. We walked out to the side in a spot I felt was secure enough from prowling eyes. I placed my hand on his house and I took a moment of silence to tune in. The first thing I picked up on was his voice and it seemed angry. He was yelling about how he thought he never had anything or any help from anyone. I do not think it was his conscious spirit but a piece of his energy. It played over and over like a broken record with residual energy. With residual activity spirits do not respond.

Over the next week I began to pick up on the fact he was not far. I began to feel he had to be in the house. I told my family he had to be in his house. This feeling kept growing and finally his sons came to clean out the house. The first day they worked on the top floor. Then the second day they started cleaning in the basement. As they worked toward the back part of the basement, they noticed a bed mattress standing up against the wall. Then suddenly they saw a shoe sticking out between the wall and the mattress. When they checked behind, they found his body in the middle. It looked he had been dead for about a week or more. This was shocking to everyone.

After his body was discovered I could feel an energetic hold on me was finally released, like I was being freed from a huge responsibility.

Caution!

There is another issue to having psychic abilities. I have learned over the years care needs to be taken about who to tell about these abilities. Not everyone is going to understand. This does not mean to deny a part of yourself or your abilities. There are some who are accepting. Many people misunderstand how these abilities work. I found this true when working psychic fairs. People want definitive answers where there are none. Other people do not believe in any psychic abilities or other worldly occurrences. It appears to be best to pick the audience, time, and place to declare and exhibit psychic abilities.

Another recommendation I have is for psychic kids and even teenagers to not talk about their abilities at school. This can raise some red flags. It is also not good for psychic adults to discuss it at their jobs. People in these environments can be very conservative in their thinking which can lead to some serious harassment.

Parents who have no experience with psychics or their abilities may have children who are gifted. Not understanding what their children are talking about they may seek professional mental counseling for the child. It is scary enough to see spirits as a child, but to be considered mentally deficient because of it is equally scary. A professional medium could help these individuals to understand their experiences and teach children how to turn on and off these abilities.

I did not tell my parents about my visions as a young child. Fortunately, by the time I revealed my abilities my parents supported me.

These alerts I have stated above are to protect us from those who do not understand. I have no intentions of denying my abilities anymore. I have figured I can still develop psychically and share, I just need to choose my audience. This book is my coming out.

Chapter 3

Family Experiences – Grandpa Cookie

To understand the context in which several additional psychic experiences occurred, it is best to provide some background about my immediate family.

One of the great memories I have as a kid is my grandfather (n my dad's side. We always called him "Cookie", but his real name was Carl. He lived in Parkville, Missouri and I would visit him on Friday evenings while my parents went out to the movies. He really was crazy about me and my sister. He never called us by our real names. It was always by our nick names he gave us as small children. He called me Poik which means "little boy" in Swedish. He called my sister Tinsy because it meant "little girl." As we grew up, he still called us by those nick names. He always had a good sense of humor, but he was not always a nice person. Both his parents died of the flu epidemic in the early 1920's. His father (my great grandfather) Carl Hjalmer was in construction and farming. He was known to be extremely strong. His wife Irma was a homemaker. Their place in the community was prominent. Carl Hjalmer was so strong he could lift a wagon single-handedly. He was known as a good neighbor. For

FIGURE 4 BETH, COOKIE, ME IN 1972

Hjalmer, he could have survived the flu. It was said he was showing improvements. I was told the doctor kept telling him to stay in bed, but he kept getting up. This is understandable when you have three small children to raise, a business to run and have always been healthy. They both died in within just a few days of each other. Irma was pregnant at the time. At their passing my grandfather Cookie was about three years of age. He also had two sisters. They all went to live with their grandfather and grandmother and a mixture of other aunts and cousins. They tried to pick up the pieces the best they could. With the mixed household, as time went on, a thread of dysfunction developed in the relationships. When he got into his teen years my grandfather "Cookie" had no effective parental figure and started to get out of control. It affected his whole adult life.

Cookie inherited his father's talent in construction. He was a master plumber and could also build an entire house himself. He had a natural mathematical ability as well as physical strength. He was not a good businessman, even though at one time he owned a hardware store. As a teen and in his early twenties, he was good looking, had a car and was somewhat wild. He smoked and drank. Cookie married my grandmother, Mary Liz, the 1940's. Mary Liz was from another prominent family in the town. Her maternal grandfather was the town doctor, who was much respected. Her

FIGURE 5 MARY LIZ

father belonged to a prominent family as well. On paper, their marriage made a lot of sense. But, unfortunately, Mary Liz, even with the pedigrees, also came from a troubled family. Her father was unable to handle alcohol and would frequently be drunk. Her mother was unable to handle it very well. As often happens, Mary Liz picked a husband much like her father.

They had three boys: my father, Carl Jr., and his two brothers, Chuck, and Ned. By the time Chuck was born Cookie's drinking had really escalated and included physical and verbal abuse and infidelity. It affected the three boys extensively. My dad was into classical music and played the Trombone. He moved after Cookie threw his trombone out the back door. My father moved out of the house in his teens to live with his grandmother Nellie (we called her "Mother Ned") because he could not take his father's abuse any longer.

Eventually my grandmother Mary Liz was raising her younger two boys and started to work on her teacher's degree. My grandfather was becoming even more abusive and did everything in his power to keep her from succeeding. She eventually started to teach elementary school and did so for the next twenty-two years. My grandmother and the two younger boys could not take the abuse from my grandfather any longer and they all moved in with my great grandmother.

A serious life change was heading for my grandfather "Cookie" in his early forties. The doctor told him to stop drinking and smoking or he would die. In fact, he had "died" when he was taken to the hospital when he was drunk. He was resuscitated. He quit drinking at that moment, but much bodily damage had been done. He increased his smoking up to about two packs a day it seemed or more. I remember when I was small, he had ash trays piled with cigarette butts and he already struggled to breathe. I remember as a kid watching him sleep in his black rocking chair. He would inhale then it would be a second or two before he would exhale. It was scary. I thought he was going to die on me at times when I was alone with him on Friday nights. He ended up dying at age 63 from Emphysema. To be with me and my sister, in his last years, he made peace with my dad and mom. He came to Sunday dinner and we would eat and play games. What I did not know at the time was my sister was also psychically sensitive. She has had several significant experiences but has chosen to limit her exposure.

Shortly before Cookie died, he was in the hospital on a respirator and my sister Beth and I were not allowed in his room for long. Then my sister decided to write him a short note on a scrap of paper that said, "I love you." She gave it to the nurse, and she started to cry as she took it in to my grandfather to read. It gave him such joy and happiness. The nurse kept the letter at the front desk to prevent it from getting lost. My uncle Chuck came in and my grandfather Cookie kept asking him "Where is the letter?" Chuck had no idea what he was talking about. He asked the nurse at the front desk about the note and she handed it to him to take to my grandfather and he died shortly after that. He was buried with the note in his suit pocket.

Grandpa Cookie did not appear to me after he died. He chose my sister Beth who was genuinely concerned about his soul being lost and not finding his way to the light. She could not go to sleep at night without first asking the Lord to help him find The Light. For the next three years she prayed every night without fail for him to find his way to heaven. At the end of the three years she was sixteen years of age, and she had a dream. In the dream, she was about three years old and grandpa was in his hospital gown and they started to walk together up my parent's basement stairs. She was holding his hand and he got younger going up each step. At the top of the stairs he was a young man in a suit and tie and smiling. Then somehow, they were at the top of a church steeple. An angel named Jennifer came down to meet them at the top of the steeple. She was a guide to help my grandfather to get to heaven. Afterwards, Beth awakened and said, "Thank you for helping my grandfather." The dream could have been an out of body experience (OBE) where her soul traveled part of the way with him. We both think the prayers during those three years helped clear him of his chains in life like Scrooge did. Otherwise I think he would have taken longer to find his way or become earth bound.

Family experiences – Thanksgiving 1995

As I was growing up, I always had a connection with animals. Through my teens and in my twenties, I started to wonder about if animals understood what was happening to them. Were they aware of the world? I started to have further spiritual experiences with animals. This experience in the year 1995 was when our family was getting together for Thanksgiving. The holiday I always looked forward to celebrating came to a halt. Even though I still ate meat and other animal products, I always felt something was not right with it at the same time. But I never thought an animal spirit would communicate its emotions to me about being dead. After this one experience Thanksgiving was never the same for me.

We were all sitting at the dinner table enjoying the meal and some deer meat got served. I never had deer meat and I decided to try some, and I held up my plate. As I was getting ready to take my first bite, I thought it looked rather rough. I noticed it was also hard to chew and it took me a few minutes.

As I was chewing, I did not really notice the taste as I was having a spiritual experience. I kept on chewing and I started to hear heavy breathing. It continued and started to get louder. I was also becoming surrounded by this breathing. At the same time, I began to get a vision of this deer we were eating. The vision was a male deer, and I could see him clear as day. The heavy breathing was to get my attention. He looked right into my eyes and I could see and feel his emotions of sadness. I believe he was aware he was dead, and his life was ended violently most likely by a human. As we continued eye contact, he told me telepathically that he had a family waiting for him. But he never got back to them and ended up on the dinner table.

Looking deeper into his eyes I was being pulled into his world of fear and having to stay out of view of humans. I began to feel guilty and I told him I was sorry for what happened to him. His face showed complete sorrow and I began to morn for the spiritual being and I could not finish my meal. I was too busy recapping what had happened to me in just a few minutes time or less. Twenty years later I can still feel his emotions. But I will never forget the look in his eyes. I wish everyone could have experiences like this one, it was immensely powerful.

Family Experiences – Grandma Mary Liz

Earlier, when my grandparents (on my dad's side) were still married with three kids living in Parkville Missouri my grandfather Cookie had a mistress and he would bring her to the house. I was incredibly surprised when I found out. I never thought he would do such a thing. The family today feels this mistress was possibly trying to get rid of my grandmother by poisoning her with arsenic, but it was not completely proven. She ended up having her stomach pumped. The arsenic had weakened her esophagus and caused her to cough chronically for the next 38 years and was killing her slowly. The result later turned out she had a hiatal hernia needing to be repaired. The doctor told her many times to have it fixed. She put it off for many years and suffered from chronic coughing. Finally, in 1996 she decided to have a surgeon repair the hiatal hernia. Suddenly complications began to arise from the surgery, and she was placed into intensive care. I remember a nurse taking my dad and me to see my grandmother. As I saw her lying there still heavily sedated. We were standing in front of her hospital bed. I could see her spirit next to her body looking right at us. Her hair was flaming bright red like it always was in her younger years and her red eyeglasses.

My senses were saying she was not going to make it, because of an experience I had earlier when I was in Arizona. I came upon some women selling stones and crystals on the side of a dirt road. This was February of 1996. There was a necklace with several stones attached to it which got my attention. They were all heart shaped. I picked it up and a speck of light flashed from it. Then a voice said to me my grandmother Mary Liz was going to pass in the same year in the month of September. I kept this message to myself and stored the stones in a safe place. While my grandmother Mary Liz was in the hospital my sister Beth was almost five months along with her first child. My grandmother was so excited to become a great grandmother, but she developed extremely high fevers and a blood clot. She died on her youngest son's birthday, September 20, 1996. Her middle son, Chuck, felt very guilty because he had insisted that she have the surgery.

At the funeral home in Parkville I was in total denial that she was no longer with us in the physical world. But I did know she was still with us in spirit. I never walked up to see her in the open casket. I wanted to remember her when she was alive. The following day when we were all sitting in her house, I noticed this energy throughout the atmosphere consisting of her presence as if she were sitting in the living room with us--even in the same chair. There were discussions about her and all the Christmas seasons and dinners there.

The last night the family got together at her house, we had a huge feast as if Mary Liz were there having one of her dinner parties. This was late September 1996. We set the table the way Mary Liz would have done herself. We ate lots of food and talked and laughed. When it was time for me to leave it was already dark. I walked out the back door and down the stairs. The weather was cooling off and the wind picked up. There was a long driveway and I parked at the far end. Once I got to my car I stood still for a moment. The presence of Mary Liz was all around the trees the bushes and in the wind. She was sad because this was our last gathering in her house as a family.

My grandmother was really into plants and she had her old back porch turned into a bright room with lots of windows. It consisted of yellow curtains and yellow carpet. All the furniture was yellow as well. Also, there was a round table with chairs and yellow pads on them. It was a very cheerful room. It also held lots of plants of different types and sizes. Those plants had long lives because of her daily care.

There was a large plant my dad took in and put in their home dining room. About a month later my mother asked me if I wanted to take it home. I put it by the doorway where it would be seen and admired all the time. After a few days I noticed my grandmother was in the apartment because I know she was telling me to take good care of the plant. When I came home from work, she would be pointing her finger at me to water this plant. I could see her bright red hair and glasses. She would move about the living room and would relate messages to me about the roommate I had at the time. She really did not care for this person or the cigarette smoke I was putting up with at the time. Her spirit is still with me as I see her often and she offers me advice and comfort.

Early experiences- My Nephew

Spiritual sensitivity seemed to pass from my sister to her son. My nephew was born the February following my grandmother's death. When he was three years old, he and my sister were in the car running errands and talking about "Grandma Mary" as they often did. During the conversation, out of the clear blue, my three-year old nephew said, "Grandma Mary had poison water, didn't she?" My sister thought she was going to wreck the car. How would a small child know anything about such a thing? She asked him how he heard about that? He said Grandma Mary had told him. My sister was convinced our Grandmother was sending us a message. The arsenic was the root cause of her health issues and eventually her death. It was not the fault of the doctor or hospital. I believe she was using her great grandson to try to absolve us of our guilt about her passing.

Family experiences – Uncle Chuck

My Uncle Chuck's life was very troubled as an outcome from his childhood abuse from his alcoholic father. He had little positive guidance growing up. I remember being told my grandmother Mary Liz would put the boys to bed early in case my grandfather would come home in a drunken rage. She would take the beatings instead of the three boys. Sometimes he would throw dinner out the back door if he did not like it or he would make the three boys eat more than they could and still made them eat more. This is just a fraction of the abuse they endured.

FIGURE 6 UNCLE CHUCK

These experiences had a horrific effect on the three boys. My uncle Chuck got the worst of it all. He had problems with drinking and smoking. He also got hooked on medications and other drugs and would sometimes take them with booze.

On a good note, Chuck was able to enjoy my sisters' kids and they loved him dearly! Every time he went to their house, they would run to the door yelling "Chucki's here!" What they would not give to yell his name throughout the house just one more time – he was wonderful with them. They were 3 and 7 when he died. To this day, they still remember him very clearly.

As Chuck always enjoyed kids, he very much wanted a child of his own. When he married his second wife, I was around eight years old in the late 70's. They were married for about three or four years. She was nice to me. She and I would sometimes flex our arms at each other to see who had the biggest biceps.

She and Chuck would argue a lot about not having any children. She was not interested in the least. Then one day when they were arguing about the subject she blurted out "I should have kept that little red headed brat." Her secret was now out. Chuck realized she had an abortion at four weeks along. She even told my mom and Mary Liz that a baby did not fit into her schedule. Chuck divorced her and the family told her to never come back. I believe if the abortion never took place then Chuck's life could have been different in a particularly good way.

When Chuck got into his early fifties, I noticed his health was not looking particularly good. His energy also felt very depleted. It was quite evident he did not take good care of himself. I remember in 2003 the family was having dinner at my sister's house for Christmas. As we were all talking, I noticed he was in poor health and I just knew he was not going to be with us much longer. As I looked at him, I heard a spirit saying the 'spring of 2004' and I saw this blackness filling up around his heart. I kept this to myself. On Sunday morning March 21st, 2004, I got a call from my sister telling me Chuck had been found dead in his house. The feeling of shock came over me and at the same moment I realized this was the third death in the family I predicted. He was only fifty- eight years old. Chuck had called someone for help the night he died. Then he decided to tell this person not to come. He made it to his car in the garage and started the motor. He then apparently realized he could not drive to the hospital on his own. He went back up this huge staircase while having a heart attack. He was trying to get back to the phone to call for help. He never got the chance to make the second phone call. He passed out as the carbon monoxide from the car filled the house. He was found the next morning when friends tried to check on him and there was no answer. The car had run out of gas and the garage door was still shut.

The next day the family was starting to clear out his house and I was starting to take his clothes out of his closet and fold them up. When I reached for some shirts and pulled them out of the closet, I saw Chuck on my left trying to grab the shirts back from me. His arm went through the shirts I had in my hand and then he vanished. His quick appearance seemed very physical, but I saw him with my real eyes. At this moment I knew he was in the house. This vision of Chuck was for about five or six seconds. He would hang out in the bedroom and the main bathroom and was wondering what we were doing going through his belongings. As the day progressed, I kept getting the feeling he was watching every move we made. Sometimes I had to go outside because I could feel his rage building up.

His energy was extraordinarily strong around this huge staircase going down to the garage. This was one big set of stairs, and very steep. I went down the steps to see what everyone was doing. As I proceeded up the stairs, I felt heavy and short of breath. Each step became increasingly challenging as I clawed my way up, grabbing on and flexing my fingers into the carpet. Chuck was showing me his last moment of life as it was. I could feel his desperation and panic. When I got to the top of the stairs I was no longer overwhelmed, but I do believe he was in my body for a moment. The shortness of breath and panic came to an end. As

I look back at this experience it seems the bottom half of the stairs is when he was on foot, but the upper half is when he fell forward and used his hands to climb up while trying to get to the phone. I felt bad for Chuck because he died alone.

Prior to the funeral services my mom got a phone call from Chuck's second wife who had the abortion, after a good twenty years. She told my mom she still felt she did nothing wrong. My mother was astounded by this message. This made my sister hire a security guard for the funeral to keep her from coming in. I do not think the family will ever forgive her for what she did.

A few days later, on a Wednesday evening the family attended the funeral home services in a small chapel. There was a nice lady minister who spoke. We all formed a single line and walked up to see Chuck in the casket. He looked like he was in a deep sleep. After the funeral I had to drive out to the Overland Park area. Walking out to my car I got a little spooked like someone was following me in a dark parking lot. I started to feel Chuck's rage really increasing as I got on the road. When I got on to the highway, it felt as if Chuck was channeling through me as he took over the car. I had no control on the gas pedal and I just froze as Chuck drove the car like a crazy person. The driver seat suddenly felt crowded. There was no doubt Chuck totally jumped me at this very moment. I avoided the rearview mirror all I could while noticing his eyes looking back at me in the reflection. He was figuring out he was no longer alive in physical body. The car kept increasing speed and I still had no control until I got off at an exit. I gained control back over the car and I expressed my anger at Chuck for putting me at risk. The next minute he was gone. I am sure he felt guilty not realizing what he had done as he would never intentionally hurt me.

The next morning was the burial in Parkville where he spent his whole life. My sister and I sang the song "Amazing Grace." I was pleased to see it was well attended. As I was watching the burial, I started to look around the graveyard. I started to look at graves of relatives who have been gone from us for many years. Our family was getting smaller and I had missed knowing these other people. Some blue funeral flowers were offered to me to take home. I hesitated on the idea as something told me to be greatly aware! I thought as I took the flowers home his spirit could follow me. Later in the night I was at home with my cat Tigress and she noticed something, or someone was moving around in the apartment. I believe animals are more sensitive to spirit activity than humans. The temperature began to increase while inside. I think it was caused by his anger. Suddenly it felt like I was in a wind tunnel. This feeling told me Chuck came home with me along with his rage and I could sense him throwing things around and screaming. As this escalated, I ran outside and called my sister Beth around 8:30pm. I told her what was going on. She got a little upset with Chuck and told him to leave me alone and to talk to her. She called me back around 10:30pm and said he was now at her house. He was still expressing a lot of anger about being dead. My place became completely quiet for the time being.

The experiences were not over yet. My last encounter with Chuck was the next morning on a Friday around 5:30 am. I was half awake and half asleep. Chuck was standing in the doorway of the bedroom and asking me "Why is this happening to me?" I told him he did not take good care of his health and as a result his life ended. This next experience was immensely powerful and sad. Chuck was starting to make his way to where he needed to be, and I assisted him part of the way. This I feel was another out of body experience. I then saw my grandmother Mary Liz meet us halfway and she began to hug Chuck as he cried on her shoulder. Mary Liz told him "It's going to be okay." He asked her, "Why is this happening to me?" She also told him he did not take good care of his health. After they both had a good cry together, I knew Chuck was gone and I never sensed him again. I hope he is happy, wherever he is. When I awakened a few hours later I felt like I had a highly active night even though I still slept. I will never forget this incident.

As the next day progressed, I had a strong feeling Chuck had crossed over to the afterlife. It was later discovered while my sister was going through his complicated estate, he had a heart valve issue and was told several years earlier by our family doctor to get it looked at. He was terrified of doctors and hospitals due to the experience with my Grandmother. But it ended up killing him. He died of Acute Pulmonary Edema which causes the valve to malfunction and fluid was backed up into his lungs. With a 95% death rate and being alone when this was occurring, he did not stand a chance. The carbon monoxide was absorbed through his skin but was not the cause of his death.

Much later in November of 2019, a close friend of Chuck's told of a behavioral pattern he had. Chuck would go down the large stairs into the garage with no shoes on, start his car without opening the garage door, then would go back upstairs and put on his shoes. This is the position he was in when he died and was the position he was in the next morning when he was found dead.

Chapter 4

Journeys to Colorado

Spending time in my childhood with my family driving out to Colorado required a trip across the state of Kansas. It was long but fun. I remember I kept on asking my parents "Are we there yet?" and my sister and I would pick on each other in the back seat.

This journey was to visit my mom's parents Frank and Vera Holmes. Frank and Vera had met in high school and married right out of college. Frank was raised on a farm in Garnett, Kansas. He decided he wanted to be a minister when he was twelve years old. Vera was raised in Greeley, Kansas. She lost her mother when she was six years old. The home life suddenly became chaotic and abusive. She made it a habit to hide from her father. He remarried six years later, and the home suddenly became "like heaven" in grandmother's words.

As a Methodist minister, my grandfather got moved around quite often. He also served in World War II as a Chaplin in the South Pacific (Guadalcanal). His presence as a spiritual leader was important to the soldiers. He was immensely proud to be a Veteran. Frank was a minister for fifty years, serving in the Rocky Mountain Conference. My grandmother

FIGURE 7 FRANK AND VERA ON THEIR WEDDING DAY

Vera taught Sunday school, taught in public school and college classes. She also took care of their home. I have memories of him chewing on a toothpick.

My mom's parents found their final retirement home in Cañon City, Colorado. It was a quiet little town. I remember visiting them in the summers. Grampa Frank had a couple of habits I remember. He used to chew on tooth pics quite often. He would also say "whee whee whee" when we came in from the outdoors. My grandfather and I would go to this Methodist camp where he worked as a counselor and manager. He filled in as a preacher at various churches to keep busy. My grandmother worked on genealogy. They traveled the States often.

In March of 1990 we got a phone call from my grandmother, Vera. She told us Frank was going into the hospital. His lungs were starting to fill up and harden. It was going at a fast rate. He was put on a breathing machine. My mom and my sister Beth got out to the hospital in Pueblo, Colorado as quickly as they could. My dad and I drove out to see Frank as fast as we could get there. When we arrived, I saw one of my cousins and my mom's foster sister Shirley who we had not seen in years. My grandmother was holding together quite well.

Grandpa Frank seemed to be showing some signs of improvement. We began to feel particularly good about this. As we started to feel a little bit of relief, my Dad and I returned home. My mom had a conversation with the doctor about it. She was hoping Frank was really going to recover. But the doctor told her he has seen these situations before. The best thing to do was to wait and see what would happen.

Grandfather's breathing became very labor intensive. For a day or two, it looked like he was doing better. It was Easter week, and he gave Easter sermon from his hospital bed. We have this on tape. My mother remembers a reader telling her to try and keep him from choking. At the time, she had no idea what that meant. But, on the second day of the Holy Week, he choked on cottage cheese and it took several hours for him to recover as he could not catch his breath. That was the beginning of the end. My sister, Mother and Grandmother took turns being by his bed side as he had become comatose. Around 2:00 pm on Lonely Tuesday, my sister took her shift and held his hand. Fifteen minutes later, he began to groan and moan, saying "NO, NO, NO." He was telling someone or something "No!" He took three deep breaths and died at that moment. It seemed he was fighting some spiritual source or heaven itself as he was not ready and did not understand why he was being taken. At the same time my mom's brother Lynn, who was driving to the hospital, felt a rush moving through him and said to Verna, his wife "I think we are too late". He knew Frank had already passed. They continued driving straight to Cañon City to meet the rest of the family.

After Frank passed, my sister, my mom, and her foster sister Shirley and her husband, Les, and Vera were all walking out of the hospital to the parking lot. Then the leaves began to shuffle with an extraordinarily strong windstorm. My sister Beth looked around and said, "Grandpa Frank is pissed!" This windstorm followed them all the way from Pueblo to Cañon City. Tumbleweeds flew across the highway in a rage as they traveled. When everyone walked into the house the windstorm quieted.

My dad called me at work to tell me "It looks like you have no more grandfathers." I got this empty feeling inside as I was standing there. When I got home, I started to get ready for the drive back out to Cañon City, Colorado for the funeral. I found myself standing in the kitchen the night before by the refrigerator. As I looked towards the sink, I could see my grandfather Frank on a psychic level standing and looking right at me. He was terribly angry, and I knew he was not going to move on without my grandmother Vera.

On the evening of the funeral wake, my sister Beth was there with my grandmother along with Shirley who was my mom's foster sister as well as Frank's sister, Louisa, and her son. During this time, my mom and I stayed behind at the house. The energy became very disturbing as Frank's presence became extraordinarily strong in the house and I said to my mom "I believe grandfather is in the hallway and in his office." As the evening progressed, we eventually had every light on in the house because his presence was so strong. He seemed to want us to leave his things alone. If we had to use the bathrooms, they were right by his office and the room we were staying in was right across from his office as well. While my mom was uncomfortable, I could not escape his anger as he roared through the house.

The next morning the family headed to the church where my grandfather Frank preached for many years. The one thing my grandfather never approved of was open casket funerals in the actual church, which was being done to him. I thought it was in poor taste. My sister noticed his wedding ring was missing. He and my grandmother had been married for 56 years! She went to speak to the funeral director and right in the middle of the service they barged in and put the ring on. I thought my sister was going to become one of the tumble-weeds that raged across the highway! But had it not been open casket that would never have been noticed. My mom and I could not look at him because we wanted to remember when he was alive.

Later in the day, my mom and I and her brother were all sitting in Frank's office. I could feel his presence again and he was getting upset because we were going through his office materials. I could see him sitting at his desk and I could hear him say "Leave my things alone!" He wanted every-thing to remain as he left it.

I was becoming unnerved more and more that Frank was guarding his office because he started to figure out that we were going to clear it out. At times I could see him going through his office to make sure everything was still in place. As a result, he would continue to stand in the hallway or he would sit at his desk, guarding everything.

As the months went on my grandmother Vera was going through a tough adjustment without my grandfather. He al-ways took care of the financial ends and my grandmother would take care of the house and cook the meals. My mom was going to make another trip out to Colorado to visit her mother and to be of assistance to her. My sister Beth was having a feeling of dread about the long drive my mom was about to make, then she decided to go with her. During the drive they were coming to an intersection in a very rural area of Kansas. As my mom started to pull out my sister said loudly "STOP" my mom came to a screeching halt. An exceptionally large truck appeared right where they would have been if my mom would not have stopped. They could have been completely run down. But thanks to my sister Beth they were both safe and she no longer had the feeling of dread. I feel a serious accident was prevented by my sister's premonition.

Another event happened during their trip when my sister Beth was in Frank's office and they were clearing out materials. There were tapes that contained his sermons from over the years plus he had several copies of the Bible. There was one specific copy my sister decided to take with her. She started to have a feeling something was wrong. When she put it in her suitcase, this feeling of being tapped on the shoulder occurred. Something told her to take another look at this copy of the bible and she noticed it had genealogical records and it was supposed to go to Frank's sister. She put the bible back in his office and took a different copy to take home and the nagging feeling was gone. She ended up saying "Oops sorry grandpa". But his sister ended up dying of the same illness he died from three years later. As of this day we have no idea where this Bible is or who may have it.

As this trip continued my sister was dealing with Frank quite a bit and as I look back, we were both having experiences with him. My sister Beth heard Vera (my mom's mom) crying in her bedroom while Frank was still walking around the house angry about being dead. He started pouting and my sister told him to stop feeling sorry for himself and go into the bedroom and make her feel better. But he was not ready to move on without my grandmother Vera. We always called them soul mates. There was a vision I had over the next nine to ten months: Before my grandmother Vera passed on, Frank was waiting for her in the distance near a bright beautiful light wearing his hat and waiting patiently.

I would see him almost every day in the distance waiting. This vision was telling me Vera was not going to be with us much longer.

FIGURE 8 FRANK WAITING FOR VERA
ILLUSTRATION BY KRISTINA MCPHEETERS

My grandmother Vera was living alone. Shirley was a great help during these months. My mother continued to make trips out to Colorado to see her. Vera began to show health problems, and someone was always with her. She was placed in a nursing home instead of homecare. My mom told me her mother would walk around in the nursing home, looking for her living room. She would walk around saying "Where is my living room?" My mother would say, "You can't get to your living room from here." Vera kept on losing weight and it was becoming life threatening. Then one day she started to say, "I hear church bells, I hear church bells." Later, we found out her health challenges, which had been undiagnosed, were already affecting her before grandfather showed any signs of his fatal illness.

During the second week of January, Shirley called my mom and told her to get out to Cañon City as soon as possible. My mother was trying to get there and got held up in Denver in a snowstorm. She checked into a motel and got a message that her mother Vera died. After she heard this my mom had an emotional breakdown. It seemed Vera was trying to hold out for my mom but on hearing she was held in Denver by snow, could not hang on any longer.

On the day of Vera's funeral, I was at home in Kansas City, and I was standing near the stairs to the basement. A sudden energy came from the stairs and I looked down and saw my grandmother Vera coming up the stairs. At this very moment I played a CD recording of the Berlioz Requiem in her memory. There must be something about those stairs – this was the second time one of my grandparents had ascended them from the spirit world.

My mother joined with the family the next day. When everyone gathered at the funeral home, it was also an open casket funeral. Everyone came to say goodbye to Vera. My mother was not able to walk down the aisle to the casket. She lost her balance in her legs and had to be escorted down. Her brother and Verna ended up carrying her down the aisle to see once and for all her mother Vera has passed.

During the funeral service at the cemetery my sister Beth had a spiritual experience when she felt the soul of Vera pass through her. Grandmother said she was happy and out of pain. This gave my sister the feeling of happiness as well. Grandfather was there to greet his wife, and they left together.

Chapter 5

Spirit Vision

As a small child it never occurred to me that talking with spirits could be anything positive. The idea of an actual spirit communicating with me directly remained very un-nerving for years. My teacher Pat would tell me in class she always saw me as very intuitive or even psychic. At the time I never thought I was an actual psychic or even had any abilities of this nature. I eventually, began to have a better understanding of what she was telling me. It started to make sense when I got my first apartment. These cases be-low are experiences I was not expecting at all, they just happened.

The Westport apartment building

In the year 1994, I made a move into the Westport area of Kansas City, which contains a good number of old buildings and houses. This was a time when this area had a lot of its original character. The apartment was perfect for me. It was on the second floor towards the back side of the building. There were two other apartments in the front of the building with balconies. This was not an excessively big building.

After a few weeks of being in the apartment I started to become a little unnerved. The environment began to change gradually as the days and weeks passed. I was becoming convinced something else was there besides the living. I could feel someone moving around in the hallway with no one there to see, but they could see me.

This feeling continued, and still, no one was there to see. I eventually got my first sighting of a spirit of a female in the hallway. I never felt threatened by this spirit, but I did feel sadness. Whenever I was in the hallway, I would feel like I just lost someone awfully close to me. Grief would surround me and the environment.

As I would notice the spirit more often, I could pick up on her emotional state of this grief. It was my impression this female spirit lost her little girl at a young age. I began to get a vision of her wearing a black dress with long sleeves with ruffles and a white shawl around her shoulders. She was very slim, and her hair was up in a ball. I figured she lived in the building in the 1930's and this would explain her appearance. There was never any communication from her. She would pace around the hallway crying while holding a handkerchief towards her eyes.

Two decades later I still have a strong sense this female spirit was hoping her little girl would come back to her. I could not see how she died but I could detect it was tragic. This grieving woman was pacing in life and waiting and still pacing and waiting in death. I do not feel the daughter ever came back to her mother. Looking back at this experience it had to be residual energy since she never communicated with me. Her pacing pattern of grief just kept on playing over like a broken record.

After a few months I was becoming aware of another spirit on the bottom floor. This was a male presence and he communicated with me directly (which I call conscious activity). This experience was a little startling with the first sighting as suddenly there he was looking right at me! During this first occurrence he was noticeably quiet. He communicated with me telepathically when he did have something to say. I remember it all very well. I could see him on an intuitive level or through my mind's eye. He had thick black hair with a five o'clock shadow. Another feature was a mustache and large cheek bones. He was wearing a white shirt with blue jeans and he had a small belly. He looked like someone in his middle 40's who lived in the sixties. As I would do the laundry, he would tell me how upset he was about being dead. The vision I had of him was crystal clear and I could see him as if he were in physical body. Almost like a movie screen.

The look he gave me was incredibly sad and I felt that he was hoping I would have answers for him. He would ask me the same question each time which was "Why did my life end so soon?" I would always have the same answer for him. He did not take good care of himself due to bad habits. This male presence could not accept the fact that he was dead, and his plans were not being fulfilled. I think new career opportunities were coming his way. Things started improving for him, but it was too late.

It became obvious this male spirit felt envious I was living in a physical body. It seemed he would try to get close to me hoping to experience the feelings of a physical body. He would try to get a little closer each time, to feel all the senses of a physical body. I picked up on blockage around his heart, which was probably the cause of his sudden death.

These two spirit energies in the building appeared to be no threat but then something else in the basement began to make itself known. There was a cold presence coming from the back of the room. It did not look human or friendly. I became uneasy with this entity. I could see a reddish black mist. I was not worried about the two human spirits, but I was worried about the dark presence on the bottom floor. This cold presence would watch every move I made. It always knew when I was coming down the back stairs to the bottom floor. When I came home from work, I would park in the back of the building and go through the back entrance. This back entrance would put me directly in front of this cold entity. It would be ready for me each time I entered the back. I eventually made a habit of going around to the front door instead which made me feel a lot safer.

This was the second black entity entering my life. I eventually had to detach myself from it. As of the male spirit in the laundry room I do not know if he ever crossed over. Maybe someone did help him. Today I would have helped him cross over and done a complete investigation. When it was happening, I never knew spirits could be investigated or helped.

After moving out of the building I thought this was going to free me of these kinds of experiences. It just moved towards more occurrences.

FIGURE 9 THE MAN IN THE BASEMENT
ILLUSTRATION BY ADAM TILLERY

Lee's Summit Spirits

I was visiting a friend who I just met at a training work-shop. This person lived in an older house with two levels in Lee's Summit, Missouri. She had me go around to the back door instead of the front.

When I walked through the back door it felt like a huge explosion of activity all around me. I immediately picked up on three spirits. Two of them I knew were relatives of my friend and I knew what gender they were and why they were there. The third entity did not make itself completely known until later in the evening. One was a female who I believe was an aunt. I saw her with blonde hair with a yellow hat and a yellow dress. It seemed to me she lived extremely comfortable in life. She was there to protect my friend from the male spirit who was terribly angry towards me. I saw him wearing a green like military uniform and he had dirt and scratches on his face and hands. He would stand behind me as I was sitting on the couch thinking he could scare me off.

I got the feeling he wanted my friend to be alone in the house. It seemed he was truly angry with her and her family-something about going to war. As the evening progressed, I would feel a supernatural cold from all the activity. I was not ready to say anything to my friend. Chaos continued to build because these spirits knew I could see them and hear them.

Shortly after, it felt a little colder when I started to hear a voice saying "GET OUT" coming from the top of the stairs. The voice sounded low and scruffy but also aggressive. It kept distracting me from the movie we were watching. Then I heard it again "GET OUT" with a mischievous laugh. This is when I realized I had clairaudience (psychic hearing). Then I noticed a set of red eyes at the top of the stairs that was staring us down. As this continued, I also picked up on activity outside of the house on the front porch. The house had large windows and I could feel spirits looking at us. I decided at around 9:30 to call it a night. I was still not speaking up on the spirit activity in and around the house. I started to hear "GET OUT" again with the mischievous laugh. I could still see the red eyes at the top of the stairs. I believe what I was experiencing was possibly a Poltergeist (crazy ghosts) which is only created by a person with long term stress. They can become entities of their own and they can attack. I do not think it was anything demonic, but they can be terrifying.

As our evening activities came to an end, we said goodbye and I walked out the back door. It was extremely dark, and there were spirits still outside the house. As I was heading home, I noticed a spirit attached itself to the car on the passenger side. It seemed like it was a prankster spirit who was laughing all the way back to my apartment. When I got home, I turned in for the night and about five minutes later I heard knocking on the kitchen window. Then I heard the knocking again and this time it got my attention. I was on the second floor and the kitchen window had no tree limbs or outside stairs. There was no way a living person could have been knocking on the kitchen window. A few minutes later the knocking happened again. I asked my roommate at the time if he heard the knocking. He said, "No I don't hear a thing." As the knocking continued, I was the only one who appeared to be hearing it. Then I realized it had to be the prankster spirit who was having a jolly time scaring me.

My mind began to spin because I had a hard time accepting the fact that a spirit banged on the kitchen window two floors above ground. My heart was beating fast through my chest. The next day when I got home from work the prankster spirit was still there. I told my sister about it and she said to claim my home and to release it. I told the spirit to leave and never come back and it left that same day. The apartment finally calmed down.

Old Spirits and the Spirit Board

In the late part of the year 1996 I was visiting some friends who live in an older neighborhood. My roommate I had at the time had a sister who was living in her aunt's house. To get to the bedrooms on the upper floor it was necessary to go out the front door and go in the door next to it. Well, one night I was on my way up there and I felt a lot of activity as I walked up the stairs. As I approached each step it felt as if someone or something was behind me. I started to get a chill when I got to the top of the stairs then I started to pick up on two spirits of a man and woman. They made themselves known to me and they started communicating telepathically. I could see them as if they were in physical body and the clothes they were wearing were in full detail. I began to see flames of fire surrounding them. In a sense I was feeling the heat coming from those flames and I was able to hear those flames. I believe that was the cause of their death and they were still claiming their house.

This older couple continued to reveal themselves to me. They stared at me with aggressive facial expressions. The husband had white hair and he was wearing a rugged white shirt and brown pants that looked wrinkled. The wife was standing behind him wearing a long-printed flower dress with flowers printed on it. Her hair was also up in a bun. They looked as if they were in their 60's and did a lot of physical work around the house. Their skin looked roughened and I saw that the male spirit had hands that were hard and dry.

When I got back down the stairs, I noticed that the two spirits were also at the bottom of the stairs. I was getting a feeling that they were saying "Don't come back" as they continued to claim their home. I never said anything to anyone in the living room what I just experienced. I do think that everyone living in the house were aware there were spirits present.

A few minutes later my friends wanted to play the Ouija board also known as the spirit board. The feeling of excitement came over me, but I also felt a little unnerved. This was my first time to use a spirit board, which another tool used for spirit communication. We all had our hands on the Planchette which was placed on the Ouija board. I remember us asking "Is this your house?" we got the answer YES. The next question was "Do you want to communicate with us?" and the answer was YES.

I began to work the board by myself which was not my intention. As I was asking questions like "Is there someone here you wish to communicate with?" the answer was YES. Then I asked, "Who are you?" The Planchette began to move towards letters that did not spell anything that was English. I started to think that they did not speak English very well. Another question I asked them was what their name or names are. Again, it was showing spelling of something not in English. I believe the couple could have been from another country.

We decided to stop due to us not being able to understand what the spirits were spelling out on the board. The thought of amazement was running in my head. My hands felt a force pulling them to the different areas of the board. I was happy to get out of that house and go home. Nothing negative ever happened after that. I do believe the spirit board can be a positive experience for spirit communication.

Everyone needs to be educated first before practicing the board, however I order to keep negative energies at bay.

In 2016 I received some information on the spirit board. Messages coming through can be extremely limited due to how the board is designed with Yes and No with the letters and numbers. It has been said by some that mostly the low intelligent spirits come through, which I do not believe.

As I reached my thirties, I was experiencing a lot of fear. This fear I could feel throughout my mind and my body. It seemed I was running away from something I could not describe. I thought I was finished with the spiritual work. I had never really believed I had psychic abilities and I still had not reconciled with being able to sense, see and speak to the dead.

After a few more years I got a sense my spirit guides were messaging me. I would be doing my psychic work and new things would arise for me to learn. I finally figured out this is what I spent the last few years running away from. A big part of the message was a vision lining out what I was supposed to be learning. It was clear I was meant to work as a psychic and a healer. I began to feel relieved with this vision. All my experiences started to make sense.

Female Prisoners (Reading)

When I started to come out of my psychic closet, I was not sure how people were going to respond. I started to open to my abilities myself and gradually with other people. I did open up to a friend of mine named Amy in Smithville, Missouri. We first met when I was organizing a fundraiser to help abused farm animals. She called me to ask if she could be of any help. She was amazed when I called her by her nick name which was "Amy" and she asked me if I was psychic. Over the months we became good friends. She asked me if I could do a spiritual reading for a friend of hers who I had met once, but I knew nothing about her.

I drove out to Smithville and we waited for it to get dark outside. I began to light candles to have a more soothing and spiritual setting. The first thing I did was to ask what her friend wanted to know. She asked about her mother. I started by going into a deep meditation and asked the spirit guides, "What are the messages I am to pass on?"

The room got quiet for a moment and I started to get a vision of female prisoners. I told my friend this and she was surprised because she already knew the mother was in prison. The next vision I got was of the mother's long blonde hair. She was dangerously underweight. Her face looked a little scruffy and she was wearing a hospital gown. I started to ask the spirits for more information. I saw the mother was not an ordinary prisoner. She was a special case being treated as a mental patient. Her cell had strict security and had many guards around her since she was known to be harmful to herself. They even watched her when she slept and ate. I also got she would not get any parole, and she would continue to be treated as a mental patient.

A few days later, the daughter decided to check on the prison and sure enough her mother was in the psychiatric ward with guards around her cell watching every move she made. She was also very much underweight. When I got the feedback, my friend said there was no other way I could have known this information except from spirit.

The next vision about the mother was of snow on the ground and right above it a thin layer of black mist floating above the snow. The trees were tall and thin and bare, the sky was dark and grey. Then I heard a strong howling wind. I got a message saying she may die during the winter season of an unspecified year. I also sense the mother was not happy.

A year later I did another reading for the daughter. This time she was present. I held a set of keys which belonged to her mother. I sat out in the parking lot where the daughter was living at the time. As I began the reading holding the set of keys the weather started to cool off and the wind started to pick up. The wind seemed to be blowing through the trees. I thought due to the timing this could have been a coincidence and or spirit (Spirits) at work.

As I continued holding the keys, I started to get another vision of the mother going in and out of consciousness. I could see her head falling back but her eyes would sometimes stay open and then she would sit back up and be fully aware of things again. It seemed it was happening to her every day. I also picked up these red gashes on the back of her legs and they were bleeding. The additional weight lost was even more dangerous to her.

A short while later the daughter came out to tell us to come on inside of the home where she was taking care of an elderly couple. On the way in my friend Amy asked me if I could do a reading on the car the daughter had in her possession which belonged to her mother. I put my hands on the top of the car and I heard a female voice screaming. Then I got a vision of a girl being pulled out of the driver's side by a man whom I had never seen. I only saw the back of his head as he grabbed the girl and dragged her across the parking lot. This was a very disturbing vision! I figured it was the daughter I heard screaming. I told my friend what I was seeing and hearing as my hands were placed on the car. Her jaw dropped and she said she had a good idea what I was talking about.

We were invited into her room and we sat down, and I began to tell her what I was getting on a psychic level. It turned out the red gashes on the back of her mother's legs were from IV injections from being underweight and they were not able to get them in her arms. The redness looked very raw and infected. I began to tell her about what I got on her mom's car and I saw a man aggressively pulling her out of the car. She told me the man was the son of the elderly couple she was taking care of and he wanted the car for himself. He pulled her out by the hair and dragged her screaming across the parking lot. She then told me she never got the car registered for this reason.

I picked up a lot of turmoil between the daughter and her mother. The mother was very demanding of material possessions. I told her no matter how much she did for her mother it was never going to be enough. I also got another vision of her trying to make peace with her mother by forgiving her for the past. But it would not make any difference to the mother. She still felt she deserved more.

The next vision about the mother was of snow on the ground and right above it a thin layer of black mist floating above the snow. The trees were tall and thin and bare, the sky was dark and grey. Then I heard a strong howling wind. I got a message saying she may die during the winter season of an unspecified year. I also sense the mother was not happy.

I picked up a lot of turmoil between the daughter and her mother. The mother was very demanding of material possessions. I told her no matter how much she did for her mother it was never going to be enough. I also got another vision of her trying to make peace with her mother by forgiving her for the past. But it would not make any difference to the mother. She still felt she deserved more and more. The last I heard the mother was placed in a nursing home and is still seriously underweight.

Spirit Travel – Lynn

During the years 2011 and 2012 my mom and her brother started to visit more with each other. I wish they could have lived closer to one another than they did. Their last few visits were important because mom's brother was having health challenges for quite some time. When she saw him in the hospital, he seemed to be making some improvement. He was sitting up and walking around. She wanted to stay up there with him, but she knew she had to go back to work.

When she returned home from her trip visiting him, she asked me if I could do a reading on his chances of surviving his health condition. This felt incredibly challenging since it was concerning her brother. I had high expectations of myself to do this reading and how I was going to approach it. But I already had a strong feeling he was not improving.

I sat down in her bedroom and I put myself into a meditative state. I called out to the spirits who would be assisting. The first thing I saw was a vision of Lynn and he was wearing a hospital gown. The next thing I picked up on was his exhaustion and him feeling the need to put up a brave front. But the big part of the reading was when I asked spirit what they could tell me about his health situation. I felt this was a huge question to ask and spirit answered with a huge vision.

When the vision was presented to me, I found myself standing at the front end of a pathway. It was very narrow looking, and it seemed like it went for miles. There was truly little light in this pathway. The bigger part of the vision was these walls that were all square shaped. They were creating the path itself straight forward facing each other. They were gigantic walls and at the top were these grey clouds. I could not see any sunshine anywhere or towards the end because I could not see the end of this path. I got the feeling nothing was possible.

A few weeks later Lynn died. I felt he deserved more time on earth to be with his family. The next thing I realized my mother was the only one left of her family she grew up with.

FIGURE 10 LYNN'S HALLWAY

When I saw her the next day, I told her Lynn was going to be having trouble realizing where he was. Plus, it would be difficult for him to learn how to let go of the physical experience and move forward in the spiritual realm. I tried to see if it were too early to do a channeling session and see if Lynn was ready to communicate. He was not ready due to dealing with the transitional process. All I got from him was a lot of anger. My mother was extremely concerned about him. He was still in his death state.

After another four to five weeks had gone by, I began to wonder if Lynn was ready to communicate. My mother came over to see me and we were both thinking it was time to check in on her brother. By this time, my channeling abilities were stronger, and I decided to see if Lynn would be able to respond. We darkened the room and I got in a comfortable position. When I got myself in a deep state of meditation, I called upon my spirit guides and guardian angels and filled the room with white light. I called out to Lynn and he took some time to respond to me. When he figured out that he could respond back to me it was mostly through telepathy, sort of speaking without words. When I started to receive messages back from Lynn, I felt a lot of exhaustion and weakness.

The channeling session got even deeper. I picked up on another presence. When I asked this presence to come forward it was this white light. This light felt like a female spirit working as a guide for Lynn and as a protector and nurse. Then a vision came through and I saw Lynn sitting on a rock and feeling like he did not have the strength to move on. He was still extremely attached to the physical experience. The guide who was assisting him was not in any specific form but was more of an energy radiating this beautiful misty white light. I got this feeling this spiritual caretaker was very devoted to Lynn's recovery in the spiritual realm. As I saw him sitting on this rock, he was working on standing up and sitting down. This guide would assist him in the process and once he stood up, he would walk with a cane.

The next experience in this session was when I asked Lynn if he could tell me anything only my mother would know. I got a vision of the two as children sitting in the back seat of a car going on a family outing. He would poke her in the ribs and tease her and she would tell him to stop and he kept on poking her and laughing. Both their parents would tell him to stop and point fingers at him. My mother told me he would poke at her and thought it was funny. Then he would get in trouble for it.

As the weeks would pass Lynn would come around me and watch everything I was doing. He was curious to know how I could talk to him from the physical world. I told him communication can take place between the two dimensions and it is an ability I have.

I told him other people have this ability as well. There is a group I go to called Spirit Circle, a meditation group that works in the dark. We talk with spirit guides and bring forward messages. He came with me and stood in the back corner and observed carefully. I felt he wanted to learn more about communication between earth and heaven. He was there at the group enough times and eventually other participants started to pick up on him as well. They also noticed he wanted to learn about how we can communicate with the spirit world. This said to me he wanted to talk with his family and let them know he is still near them.

As he got stronger his guide was still with him but did not have to assist as much. Then I noticed his visits to me were not as frequent. I started to think he was visiting with his family. After a couple of months, he began to make his presence known again and would at times come to spirit circle.

Another vision came to me of him and my mom when she was a teenager. It was a moment of giving I picked up on first and it was something he wanted her to have because he was going to be leaving. It was a space she would be able to occupy for herself. This felt like a nice offering. My mom told me that when he left home for college, her brother gave her his bedroom because he knew how much she valued her privacy.

As the weeks and months passed Lynn got stronger and became more independent in the spiritual realm. I think he visits between my mom and his family. He also keeps coming to spirit circle. It seems to me he is still trying to figure how to communicate with the living.

Spirit travel - Uncle James

In the year 2013 my mom said she was going to a funeral. I asked her who died, and she told me it was her uncle James. He was not talked about very much and I do not ever remember being around him as a kid. I wish I would have gone with her, but the idea did not come to me soon enough. Funerals have always made me feel uncomfortable. I remember being a pall bearer for my uncle Chuck and my grandfather Frank. When she returned home from the funeral, she had a program from the service. When I paid her a visit the following evening, she handed me the program. When I saw the cover, my jaw dropped. The photo of her uncle James looked just like her father Frank who died back in 1990 at the age of eighty. James was a younger brother of Frank. There was never any talk of James that I can recall. I made a comment that he was a thin version of her father. As I continued to look at the photo it seemed like he was staring at me into my own eyes.

I started to wonder if his spirit was with us as my mom and I were talking about him. His photo gave me the feeling to check in with him to see if he was near. Looking over his name at the top of the program I began to run my fingers over the letters to create communication. As my fingers continued to move over his name, I started to call out to him. It took a few minutes, but I do feel he began to make his presence known.

The next thing I said to my mother that I thought he was in the room with us. The room began to feel different. I formed a mind plan as to how I could get confirmation that it was her uncle James. As communication continued, I started to ask him if he was happy with the results of his own funeral. The feeling I got was he was satisfied but he was not terribly excited. This showed me the possibility he was neutral about a lot of things in life. I told him my mom was going up to Washington State to visit her brother since they have not seen each other in quite some time. All I heard on this was "Oh that's nice". My mom was not surprised his comments were limited. I told her I got the sense he did not communicate a lot in life and kept to himself. The very next thing my mom said was "That's why I never visited him very much" and he was always keeping to himself.

As he was fading away, I heard him say "good luck." This was a short reading. I do believe I made contact with him. I also got the feeling he had a hard time believing the living could communicate with the spirit world. The room returned to its normal energetic flow and we never heard from him again. I do believe he crossed over on his own.

Astral Friend

In the winter of 2007, I was still living in the midtown area. One snowy day, I was walking my dog, Taylor. When we reached the front lawn, I noticed a lady walking up the street with her dog. We introduced ourselves to each other. Her name was Gita. And we let our dogs socialize for a few moments. I told her I was a dog groomer, which was my occupation at the time. From then on, we became well acquainted. We began talking about the animal rights movement, and the fact I was completely vegan. She asked me if I could groom a dog for her, a Siberian husky. He was up for adoption at the time and Gita was getting him prepared for the process by finding him a home.

Over the next two years of our acquaintance, I would walk my dog with her dog. They would sniff out the entire neighborhood in all types of weather. In the summer of 2009, Gita was managing an apartment building across the street from me. She was beginning to make comments on how tired she was feeling. As time passed into the fall season, I was hearing less from Gita. The little I did hear from her was she was not feeling well. Then about three weeks to a month later I got email from I thought was from Gita. But it was a friend of hers. She brought forth the sad news of Gita's unexpected passing over the weekend. I was shocked and grieved with this news. The words repeated like an echo "Gita is gone". I offered to take in her dog, but Gita's friend was going to take of her.

About a week or two later, I had a dream. This dream I believe was in the astral plane. I was walking my dog Taylor down the street. It was dark and cold. As we were walking, I heard footsteps behind me. These footsteps began to go faster. Then I could hear the breath and rustling of a winter coat. This person caught up with me, and I looked back. It was Gita coming up to me. She was her usual energetic self. She struck up a conversation. "Hi, how is it going?" I said "Great, just walking Taylor." She said, "That's nice." Then she asked me a question, "I hope you're not mad at me for leaving?" I said "No, I'm not." Then Gita said "Good." Then she asked me one last question "We are still friends?" I said

"Absolutely." Gita said, "Good, I am glad." Then I awakened from the dream and I realized Gita came to say goodbye.

Animal spirit

My belief in the souls of animals is based on experiences. Quite often a lot of animals get run down on the roads by drivers. They are often left there for days.

I was visiting my parents one Sunday afternoon. While driving in on Highway 9 into Parkville MO, I passed a gas station. By the entrance was an exceptionally large dog on the side of the road. The dog was a St. Bernard. The dog was lying dead and not one person took an interest. They just drove in and drove out. I made up my mind to check on him when heading back into midtown. I was at my parents for about three or four hours. While I was there, I kept thinking about the dog. Then it was time to start heading back to midtown. I drove up on highway 9 and came to the gas station. The dog was still there-- lying there dead.

I pulled over to the side of the road and made a phone call. It was to the people who pick up animal bodies on the roads. They said they would send someone out to pick up the body. I looked at this beautiful creature that most likely had a family on a search. I hope they got word of his passing. It looked to be a hit and run. Then I continued my drive home and got a vision of this dog. His soul was running with happiness. He was happy because I took time to call for his body to be picked up. Then I felt tears as I mourned for this dog. My vision of him running with happiness also showed he was out of pain.

The next morning, I made a special drive back to the gas station. I was incredibly pleased as his body had been picked up and taken care of.

In fact, several of the dogs we have had in our family have visited me after dying. Our first dog came to see me several times before he traveled on to his heavenly destination. Sometimes animals are confused by where they are and need a little guidance to move on—just like people.

Psychic Challenges

Psychic readings can be challenging work. When I finally embraced my abilities instead of running, I started giving readings. I took all the tools I learned from Pat and other teachers. I realized I wanted to enhance my channeling abilities because I felt I was being pulled in that direction. Months passed by and I was still looking for a teacher who could help me advance my abilities. A friend of mine told me of a workshop about doing channeled readings. We both took the workshop and it was a full day event. There are a lot of energies to be aware of when you channel. A channeled reading is when the psychic medium allows a spirit to enter his body. This can be a huge risk if you do not protect yourself. Bad spirits or tricksters can get into your body or at least your life. Then you would have to cleanse your body and your soul to clear out negative spirits.

I will say channeling can have its rewards. A channeler is also connecting with spirits of loved ones or spirit guides to bring forth messages. After the workshop, I decided to make some changes to what I was taught. I noticed my visualization skills advanced quite a bit since the workshop.

When I start a channeled reading, I ground and center myself. This is connecting to the earth and heavenly energies. It is also important to build a protective barrier around yourself. The way I do it is to visualize the color violet surrounding me completely. Then I picture myself waking into a bright crystal cave. Then I come to these three crystal steps going downward, towards a tall mirror showing me as I truly am. It may show me in a ritual like robe at times. Then I turn to the left and walk through a doorway. This takes me into the space I will talk with the spirit of the person I will be reading for. This is when the reading truly begins. I first describe the guide to the client. I have channeled in deities, faeries, and arch angel Michael. Sometimes the guide will be just an energy. There is no specific shape or gender. The channeling took place when I gave the spirit permission to sit in my body. I remain in somewhat control just to keep myself safe. This way I can remember more of the reading at the end.

As I began to take on more channeled readings with people, I started to experience bad headaches. This seemed very odd. These headaches got worse as I kept doing the channeled readings. I had to seek out help on this issue with other readers. We would discuss the headaches after channeled readings. It turned out it was my crown chakra which is placed at the top of your head. It is the energy center where our souls travel out and in during out of body experiences. In my case, my crown chakra was closed. I had to start working on balancing out all seven of my chakras starting at the tailbone up to my head. After a month passed, I notice the headaches were decreasing after channeled readings. It is particularly important to stay physically and spiritually healthy to do this kind of work. When I would work the psychic fairs, I would have all kinds of energies around me for the entire day. I had to make sure I was centered and well protected. I found I prefer a much quieter environment to do readings. When giving a reading, it is personal. People do not need to hear each other's readings.

Soul Healing Work

My spiritual work also took me in another direction with healing. The healing system is called Reiki. A lot of people know the word, but they do not know what it is. Reiki is an energy all around us in the universe. It is not created by the practitioner. Reiki can also be referred to as a life force that is unlimited in healing and taken in by the environment – earth-sun-moon-stars. The practitioner is merely a facilitator to bring the force to the client. The tradition of Reiki I l earned is called USUI Reiki. Usui brought Reiki into the modern world.

Usui began to study this life force when asked by students if healing by placing a hand on someone could heal them. After many years of searching to find the secret of hand healing, he finally went to a mountain known to be a sacred place for meditation and prayer. He fasted, except for water, for 21 days to try to capture the secret of this force. As the end of the 21 days approached, he was suddenly struck by a light and the secret of Reiki appeared before him. From then on, he taught this secret to those who could receive it. The power and energy are passed on from teacher to student. When the power and energy is received it is said the practitioner is "attuned." There are degrees of attunement. Attunement is a cleansing of the spirit, emotions, and soul of the practitioner. Students learn to create a clear path through their spirit, emotions and soul that allows the force to reach the client.

This healing energy can be called upon in different ways. Starting with prayer and working with meditation, visualization affirmations and intent.

To really learn Reiki, I found a teacher who taught the Usui method. I felt very honored to learn this system of healing. I believe the healing energy of Reiki can heal not just the body, but the soul. It can be done with hands on the client or with hands off.

In my early years of physical healing, I started to know other people who were already doing Rieki. I figured out it was more spiritual. What the healing source was, I had no idea. Being partially skeptical at first, I still had a curiosity about it. I remember seeing some charts of how to apply reiki, but I still had no idea how it was being done. I noticed it was being performed hands on or off. Then when I learned later it was healing the soul, I became determined to learn it. It took me a long time to find a teacher who was qualified to teach me. One night in January of 2012, I attended a meditation meetup. I met a woman there who read from a book on Reiki to the group. At the end of the evening, I asked this woman if she could teach me private lessons on Reiki. She had me come to her house for the first class, and it was exciting from the beginning.

The first book I was introduced to is called The Magick of Reiki. It is full of history and excellent instruction. I studied at her house for almost a year for first degree. The most difficult part for me was trying to understand I was not creating the energy. My teacher had to keep repeating to me the energy already exists in the universe. When I started reading the assigned book, I began to gain sacred knowledge of healing. I became even more determined to be a Rieki practitioner. Eventually, she had me bring friends over to the lesson for me to work on while she observed. I set a healing table up for them to lie on.

I learned first to start at the feet and move up the body slowly. I called upon the energy to enter my body, to the recipient by standing with my hands reaching to the sky. Feeling a current move through me and my hands heated up. Then with a vision, I saw the energy moving as a blue light. This was amazing to me to learn. There are times during a session, when I can pick up on what is happening with the body. One time in a workshop on Reiki, I told another student of an injury in her ankle from a car wreck, she told me it was from a car wreck. I can pick up on emotions and if the chakras are closed or open. I get a lot of issues with people's knees and when energy is stuck somewhere in the body. The next thing I learned in Reiki, was people thinking I can wash away all their problems and challenges in one session. It does not work like that. It could take multiple sessions for some people. Some folks are closed off and cannot receive Reiki.

When it came time for me to be attuned for first degree, I realized I was about to become a practitioner. I sat in front of my teacher and she worked with the energy and certain Reiki symbols. It took less than thirty minutes. When the attunement was over, I wondered what was going to come of it. The next day I thought I was coming down with a head cold, but it was what is called the psychic flu, which is the body cleansing itself. I endured this experience for about a full week or so. Then we took a break for a short while. But I continued to practice on friends and family.

It was time now to start second degree; there was more material to learn. This took almost a year to complete. But I remained highly determined to succeed. During the attunement process, I felt my emotions coming to the surface and breaking down. This had a raw feeling to for a while. It was intense for the first couple of weeks. But it took place for quite some time. A few months later, I started on third degree, which took me to the master level. Reiki Third Degree practice is when I learned to do attunements to pass this knowledge and power. I studied third degree with another teacher who is a friend of mine. We got third degree finished in less than two weeks. This is a powerful attunement; it is cleansing your soul. Now I have completed all three degrees of study. I still enjoy practicing Reiki on friends, family, and clients.

Another exciting experience was learning distance Reiki. Since it has a hands-off approach, I can send the energy to anyone and any distance, using their name or a photo, even a description as surrogate. I have even done distance Reiki online. When I was teaching yoga a few years ago, I had a student who was not feeling well. I asked him if would give me permission to send him Reiki, and he welcomed the idea. Since I already knew what he looked like, I used that as a surrogate. Later in the evening, I focused on his name and sent him the energy. At the end, he said he felt much more relaxed and more comfortable. I also sent distance to my sister, who was feeling a lot of stress from her job. She said it made her feel at peace with herself. These are signs when someone is open to receiving this healing energy.

Spirit Orbs

In the year 2005, my life made another turn. I attended a film festival with my yoga teacher. We saw a documentary film in the animal using business featuring all the horror and heartbreak these animals endure due to uninformed humans. A special sanctuary rescued these animals every chance they got. After the showing, we were in shock for several months trying to figure out how we could be of help to the animal rights movement. One was to go completely Vegan. The following spring of 2006, I attended a Gala event in New York City. It was to raise awareness and funds for the sanctuary where these animals lived. There were speakers and even celebrities also attended.

The next day I traveled to upstate New York to see the sanctuary. I was up there for about two full days. I was amazed at the place. It was clean and professionally managed. These animals were safe from harm. During my future visits, it was heart breaking to see some of these farm animals still scared of humans. However, some began to trust again. I volunteered to help them raise money and awareness here in KC. I did get to attend a 25th year celebration at the sanctuary in 2011. During my visit, I wanted to document my experience with photographs. I was amazed at what I found in a few of the photos.

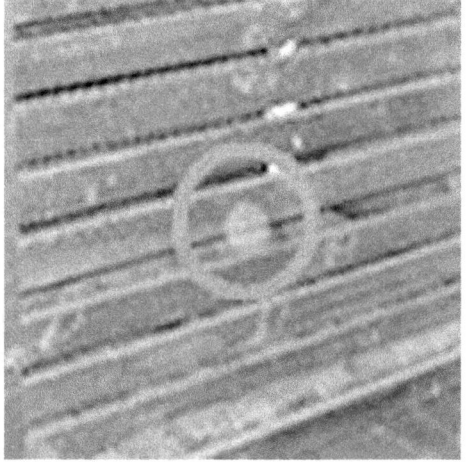

FIGURE 11 ORB ON A CRATE

When I was going through the photos, I did not see the orbs the first time. I had to go through them many times before I saw them. They appear as circular shapes. It was an extremely exciting moment to see spirit orbs of what I think are animals. To me, this is proof of the very fact animals have souls like humans. Their souls can also be earthbound. I feel these animal spirits still live at the sanctuary because they loved it in life.

Chapter 6

Group Investigations

After all my experiences through the years I decided to go and find the entities instead of waiting for them to come to me. I started to get into paranormal television shows about hunting down ghosts and psychic mediums talking with the dead. I started to learn about the tech equipment used in these kinds of investigations to get evidence of actual paranormal activity, such as cameras filming in the dark or thermo cams detecting temperature changes. My favorite is the EVP (Electronic Voice Phenomenon). With this equipment spirit voices are recorded, which may not be heard by the human ear. I did learn and experience when an area becomes cold it could mean a spirit is trying to manifest itself. After many months of watching these paranormal shows I began to wonder if there were any ghost hunting groups in Kansas City. I started to search on the internet, and I found a group called "Premiere Paranormal Research" (PPRKCMO). I signed up for my first paranormal investigation. In all my paranormal investigations I was with a group except as noted.

Haunted Historical Houses

FIGURE 12 ALEXANDER MAJORS HOUSE

Alexander Majors Historical House

The night finally came, and the weather was perfect for this event. It was dark and cold with a little bit of rain. This was a Saturday night November 19, 2011. There was also a steady breeze that made the night even more perfect. I pulled into the parking lot next to this historical house and barn. I walked into the main office inside the barn and met the team who was putting on the investigation. We started off with a good talk. They showed us a video called "Ghost Hunting 101" and then they showed a video of their previous investigation at another Historical House which I am going to be describing later in this chapter.

As we were walking around the front of the house in the cold and the wind with small flashlights, I kept looking at the large windows of the house thinking or expecting to see a ghostly face looking back at me. This was about 8:30pm. I had a feeling the house was talking to me as if it knew we were coming. The investigation team started to take in equipment to document activity and had everyone divide into three groups. When I saw the inside for the first time it looked like something out of an old Vincent Price movie. There was an old painting of a young man facing the main entrance, but I had no idea who it was at first.

This was for sure a 19th century house with old wooden floors which looked like they were still in good shape but were creaky in places. There were old pictures on the walls and a large fireplace. Afterwards, the ghost hunters broke up into three groups. The first group I was with headed up the stairs which seemed narrow. And some steps felt uneven. When I got to the top of the stairs there was a portrait of a baby on the wall and there were mannequins with period dresses on them from the late 19th century. They had long sleeves with ruffles and lace around the neck lines. As the group walked through the house in the dark there were mannequins which were shadowy. They looked like persons standing there and the thought occurred that, "It's a ghost!" But it is not. It was very startling!

We started to investigate in the main bedroom by sitting on the floor. No one could sit on the furniture. Recorders were turned on and the investigators started to ask questions like "Why are you still here?" "Is there someone here with you?" I believe by asking questions activity can be increased. The one thing I learned in paranormal investigations there is a lot of waiting around. After the group quieted down, we heard a male voice (HAAaaaa) and I said, "Did you hear that?" My jaw dropped to the floor. That alone made it all worth it. Then I heard footsteps coming in the opposite entrance to the main bedroom and coming around to my right side. I heard these footsteps as if someone were trying to tiptoe through the room without being noticed. It sounded like footsteps of a man, or the bottoms of a pair of men's dress shoes from the 19th century.

I welcomed the spirits to sit with us and talk. The spirit in the room felt male and he made the (HAAaaa) sound and the footsteps. If it was this male spirit, I think he was having a little fun with it.

As we walked through the manor again, I saw this white shape in one of the corners and I reacted very intensely and realized it was one of the mannequins with the 19th century dresses on them. That happened several times through the night.

After an hour passed by the three groups switched out rooms and my group headed down to the basement--Yeah, the basement. Someone said they were touched in the basement earlier in the night and I wondered if I was going to get touched. We had to go down a very narrow staircase. Only one person at a time could go down into this dark basement. When everyone got down the steps, we all sat on the floor and I decided to sit in one of the corners and I heard something, or someone sit next to me but there was no one there. We had little light from a video cam and that is how I knew no one was there sitting next to me. But someone did sit next to me not in physical body. I ended up moving away from that corner a slight bit.

Some of the photos I took showed actual orbs of spirits and I think they were people who lived in the house during their lifetime in the late 19th to early 20th centuries. Some of them could have been spirits just passing through. I did feel there was nothing to be afraid of in the house.

We headed back up to the master room and sat on the floor and this time the experience was a little different. I felt a male spirit was for sure in the room with us. A vision of a male spirit from the waist up with a black beard appeared to me in the back of the room. I am not sure if anyone else noticed it. Then I found some photos displayed of the former house owner in a suit and I noticed he looked the same as what I saw.

FIGURE 13 ORB IN BASEMENT NEXT TO THE STAIRS

The one eerie thing was going back up those narrow stairs one at a time and hoping the person at the end of the line had no spirit behind them. Then our group returned to the master room where we started. I wondered about the male voice from earlier and within minutes I heard an (AAHHHH) and it was the same voice and I think he wanted to be heard. This time it was lighter sounding.

Then everyone started to head back to the barn and a few people remained behind and we started to watch the monitors that were showing the different areas of the house. You could see orbs but sometimes it is dust. You must be careful with this issue because not everything is paranormal.

An Orb is a spirit and they are supposed to be perfectly round and with a circular design in the center. Sometimes you can see faces and they can expand into human shapes to make themselves more known. Orbs also move in certain direction. Dust does not move in any specific direction. In this book I will be showing photos of what Orbs look like.

About three months later I returned to this historical house to take some photos. As I was walking around the front of the house I started to pick up on an energy. It was female and between the ages of two and eight. This continued for a while as I took photos of the side of the house. The same energy was still with me. I also sensed a childlike laughter and this energy was moving around the house in a very playful manner. Several months later I got the EVP evidence from the investigation and I heard a little girl voice on there saying "Mamma, Mamma" and that voice I heard in more than once from the EVP's. I also heard the male voice going

(AAHHH) on the EVP and that voice I did hear with my own ears on the night of the investigation.

I have not found anything on the little girl, but I think she lived there after the year 1910 when sections were added on to the house by a man named Louis Ruhl who purchased the estate in 1904. He added on to the house in 1910 and made it into a school and then a church. I started to wonder since it was a church at one time, they might have had funerals there and this could explain some of the paranormal activity and unmarked photos.

In the fall of 2014, I returned to the AM house and attended another investigation open to the public. The group was taken up to the second floor. In one of the bedrooms there was a table set up for a séance. Even though I knew there was not much time for a real séance. The cards and candles were set up and the guide chose me from the group to sit at the table. The guide began to ask the sprits to make their presence known. This felt like a show rather than the real deal. As I sat in the chair listening, I was approached by a woman in a white dress. It had long sleeves and her hair was black and up in a ball. She came storming up to the table at me in full rage. Her face looked cross and she said, "I am sick and tired of all these people". Her presence remained for about a minute then she faded away like magic. It was amazing to experience and somewhat startling. It has come to my attention some of the spirits are tired of being contacted. But we keep investigating because the living is curious to see what is beyond death.

The painting on the wall of the young man I learned was Alexander Majors. I think it could have been his spirit with us in the master bedroom. He married his first wife Katherine Stalcup in 1834 then he married his second wife Susan Dudley Wetzel in 1857. Susan divorced AM after his business with the Pony Express fell under. He was found later in North Platte Nebraska penniless. He eventually died there at age 86 in 1900. His grave can be found at the Union Cemetery in Kansas City MO.

On the tour I was noticing this photo of the mother and child. It was said the child in the picture is dead and the eyes were added in to make it look life like. This is called post-mortem photography, mostly done in the 19th century. I think it was the idea to capture loved ones as if they were still alive. Sometimes it was the only photo taken of a certain member of the family. What I understood was it was done commonly with children.

FIGURE 14 THE WORNALL HOUSE

Second Location – John Wornall Historical House

My next place to research was the John Wornall house which is about ten minutes from the Alexander Majors house. John Bistow Wornall built the manor in the year 1858 for his second wife Eliza. The house was used as a hospital during the Civil War. Both Confederate and Union soldiers were treated there after the Battle of Westport. One of the rooms on the lower level was the operating room. The feeling of death was overwhelming. People died in there and lost limbs that were piled up outside the window. This would go on daily. I had no knowledge of such things taking place in the house. I got permission to do a walkthrough of the house on a Sunday. This was my first investigation on my own. The first room to enter was the master bedroom. This space felt as if a woman spent a lot of time in there while suffering emotional heartbreak. Then I proceeded through the hallway that passes by the staircase to the lower level. A mannequin sits in the corner with a period outfit from the early 19th century. This is also by the door going out onto the balcony to the right.

Through this hallway I went into the children's room and within seconds I felt incredibly sad and the room felt a little cold. I got a sense many children passed on and the mother was still in mourning. I figured these children were extremely young when they passed on. I spent a good amount of time in this room. Then I decided to walk down the staircase and it seemed like I was walking through a lot of energy--almost like a wind tunnel. Then I felt very sure spirit activity was taking place, so I sat down and just took it all in. As I was feeling the space I picked up on a soldier. He did not communicate back to me. It seems he was in a residual state. Residual activity is an energy pattern left behind from the actual person when they pass on. This soldier was wearing a Civil War uniform with a tall black hat and a black Yellow strap going down the front. He was also holding a rifle and he was standing in the corner of the staircase still on duty.

As I got to the bottom of the stairs, I turned right into the family room. This room seemed the most active of the entire house. It was dark and I kept picking up on the color red. I could also smell cherry like tobacco, even though no one today can smoke in the house. As I was standing there, I knew someone was in the room with me.

I suddenly felt a male energy in the room with a lot of anger. A vision came to me of a man with a blood-stained bandage going around his forehead. He was standing between the fireplace and the closet door. I sensed that he could have died in the operating room when it was a hospital during the Civil War. This wounded spirit was asking me why I was there. I felt like I needed to answer him, and I said that I was documenting my experience there. I also told him that I was deeply sorry that his life was cut short at a young age. This feeling of dread came over me because so many people have died in this room.

When I entered the parlor, it was a very peaceful. I could sense that people were having fun here as this was where guests were entertained. I picked up on a female energy around the grand piano that sits in the parlor.

The next step was to ask questions with a pendulum. The pendulum is a tool used for spirit communication when asked a Yes or No question. The first question I asked was "Would you like to be remembered in my writing project?" The pendulum began to move in a clockwise direction and I never trained it to do that. But clockwise which means 'yes' was a good sign to me. Then I asked, "What keeps you here in this house?" At that point, I began to see visions. John Wornall looked right at me and said that he felt the need to protect the house from vandalism and also said, "It's still my house." As far as he was concerned it was still the Civil War and the Battle of Westport. He seemed very assertive about it as well. I learned later that he did have to protect the house during the Civil War against vandalism.

I returned to the Parlor room where Mr. Wornall entertained guests and this is where I felt Roma would play the piano. This room is so beautiful, and it has a bright energy that I could sense the past activity of people being entertained. But not so with the family room and I headed back over to that room to see what more I could get. The same male entity was still in the same location and I could smell the cherry like tobacco. I felt so cold in this space, but I toughed it out and walked into the back area that lead into the dining room. It may have been used as a recovery room

FIGURE 15 FACE IN ORB AT BOTTOM OF THE STAIRS AT THE WORNALL HOUSE

for patients during the Civil War. As I moved back through the family room again, I continued to smell the cherry tobacco. This time I paid attention to it and got a feeling that it was connected to a male energy. I learned later that John Wornall smoked a pipe with cherry tobacco. There have been claims of the cherry tobacco being noticed by visitors in different parts of the house.

I furthered my walk through, and the letter M started to come to mind. I asked a question with the pendulum if the letter M was the first letter of a first name that belonged to a female. The pendulum moved in a clockwise direction which means 'yes'. My next question was if that name was one of John Wornall's wives? The pendulum moved clockwise again. I gained knowledge that the letter M stood for John's first wife Matilda Polk. She died within a year of their marriage (1851) with no children. All these communications were extremely exciting for me.

His second wife, Eliza Shalcross Johnson, married John Wornall in 1854. Eliza was born on April 20, 1836. She had seven children in their marriage. Her first child was a son named Frank who did live to be an adult. Her next five children, all girls, died young. Her last child out of the seven was also a son named Thomas who grew to be an adult. Eliza passed away at the age of 29 one week after Thomas' birth July 5, 1865. It seems her spirit never left the house. While I was standing in the children's room, I put my hands on the bed post and closed my eyes and I could hear her dress rustling through the room. She was wearing a long black dress with her hair up in a ball. She was in a deep state of grief. I think she feels confined to the children's room because of the loss five baby girls. She was also holding a white cloth and was wearing a shawl around her shoulders as she paced the room. I sensed that John Wornall would just stand at the door of the children's room because he could not face the sadness there.

During another public paranormal investigation in October 2012, I was standing in the children's room. I started to feel a cold spot coming up to my shoulders. It felt like a human spirit trying to manifest. I started to think it had to be Eliza trying to acknowledge us of her presence. At that moment I realized she was communicating. Running my hands through the cold spot it felt human shaped. This experience only lasted for a few minutes, but it was amazing and that is what makes paranormal investigations rewarding.

Another situation I picked up on with Eliza was her feelings toward her Cousin Roma. After the death of Eliza, John married Roma Johnson who was younger than Eliza. While I was looking over photos of Eliza, John and Roma I felt that Eliza disagreed with her cousin Roma being married to John. I picked up on a lot of friction on that issue. Eliza was not happy about the marriage. I felt it had to do with age.

Roma had four children with John Wornall and two of them were boys, John, and Charles. The other two children died young. That made a total of 11 children and only four of them survived into adults. From my understanding John got Roma the piano. My guess is she would play music during parties. Roma passed in the year 1933.

One other experience I had was out in the garage area by the garden. Some of the history I got was of a man who worked there as a chauffeur for many years. I was told he was not always a nice person. He was arrogant and prejudice towards women. The area he was mostly spotted in was the garage out back. I was given permission to go out back and pull up the garage door. When I walked in, I began to look and noticed a staircase to the second level.

As I walked around and observed I got a sudden feeling of rage and a set of eyes triggered right at me. I stood at the bottom of the staircase and I thought of going up there to take more photos. The feeling of rage increased as I walked towards the staircase. I started to put my foot on the first step, and I was warned not to enter the upper floor. This spirt was very adamant that I stay below, as if I was intruding on their space.

During another investigation event I attended in October 2013 I went in the garage with one of the team members. He was telling us that this spirit would make banging noises on the upper floor. He would then make banging noises on the lower floor if anyone did go up the stairs. Well, I knew this spirit was in the garage with us, but this team member was very scientific and tended to debunk everything. I started to get very annoyed with this person and I wanted to tell him that the male spirit was in there with us. I was told this male spirt seemed to more enjoy pulling his pranks on females who worked there rather than a group of investigators.

I believe spirits will communicate when they are given acknowledgement. It is also to my belief that if someone does not believe in them, they are not going to respond.

FIGURE 15 ORB AT WORNALL HOUSE GARAGE STAIRS

FIGURE 16 POSSIBLE SPIRIT

FIGURE 17 HARRIS-KEARNEY HOUSE

Harris-Kearney Historical House

The 1855 Harris-Kearney House in Westport was acquired by the Westport Historical Society in 1976.

The Harris-Kearney House was owned by Col. John Harris and his wife Henrietta and they had a daughter Josephine. John Harris passed in 1873 and the house was then owned by Col. Charles E. Kearney who was married to his daughter. His mother-in-law lived with them until she passed in 1881. The Kearney family lived in the house for twenty-eight years.

The house was moved from its original location in 1922 in two sections to its current location in the Westport area.

The Harris-Kearney House is a place of history to visit. My first visit was amazing, and I was not expecting anything that day. It started with going to the house in late September 2013. When I pulled up it was a little larger than I thought it would be. As I was approaching the stairs to the front porch to ring the doorbell a force stopped me in my tracks, and I felt a presence behind me. I turned and looked to my right and saw nothing. Then I turned again to my left and I suddenly saw a man in uniform that looked like he was from the Civil War times. I saw he had a gray beard. It was noticeable he was not wearing his hat. This male presence was a lieutenant. He was still on duty and keeping people from going into the house. My impression of him was he had to protect the house and the people in it. It seemed he was given that responsibility. It was not a question that he was conscious and was able to communicate with me.

The expression on his face was saying to me "You are not going in the house." He had an incredibly determined look, even with a little bit of anger. In that moment I got a good look at him. He had gray hair and a gray goatee. He had very thin hair on top of his head. The facial features contained thick cheek bones and a wide nose. The eyes were dark brown, and he had a thick jaw line. His entire face seemed slight round shaped. I would say he was around 55 years old or so. It looked as if he was holding his hat in his hands.

When I finally hit the doorbell, I was welcomed into the house. From what I was seeing, it was kept up very well and everything was nicely arranged. It was like stepping back into the 19th century. When I walked through the house and then back to the front room, I passed by very grand looking stairs that lead to the upper floor. I picked up on a female spirit who was in a long white dress with long sleeves and her hair up in a ball. I felt very peaceful with her and she was looking at me from the top of the stairs and she seemed curious to who I was. She remained in my mind for the rest of that day. On my way home I was going over the experience that I just communicated with two spirits in such a short time.

On my second visit I was attending a paranormal investigation that was arranged by the historical society open to the public. They invited in a paranormal investigation team and they were doing a lecture as part of their introduction. I was incredibly pleased to see they had a psychic on board since paranormal investigations and psychic skills go hand in hand.

We got a chance to walk around the house and take photos. I learned that a digital camera could take better photos than a cell phone can and the same with EVP recorders that capture spirit voices. I then walked through the dining room to climb the grand staircase that lead to the upper floor. I felt this was my chance to see who the female spirit was in the white dress. So, I walked up the staircase and I felt I was being guided to her photo on the wall in the children's room. My jaw dropped and I thought to myself with amazement "There she is." She had on the white dress and her hair was up in a ball. I knew it was her and that was confirmation for me.

In one of the bedrooms they used the flashlight method by asking the spirit to turn on the light and to turn it off on command. Every time the spirits would turn on the flash

FIGURE 18 LADY AT THE TOP OF THE STAIRS

they are thanked. They are then asked to turn it off, they are thanked again.

When the light turns on it means 'Yes' and when it turns off it means 'No'. We got a lot of communication that night with the flashlights. The group asked typical questions such as, "Are you a male or female?" "Did you once live in this house?"

During the investigation at the Harris-Kearny house it got cold and I wondered how late we were going to be there. The entire house was like an ice box and it got dark early that evening. I think the paranormal investigation team did a genuinely nice job taking people through this kind of research. It is important to let the public know that there is nothing to be afraid of and that these spirits were once in a physical body. But it is a good idea to still protect yourself during paranormal research and to let the spirits know you are not there to hurt them.

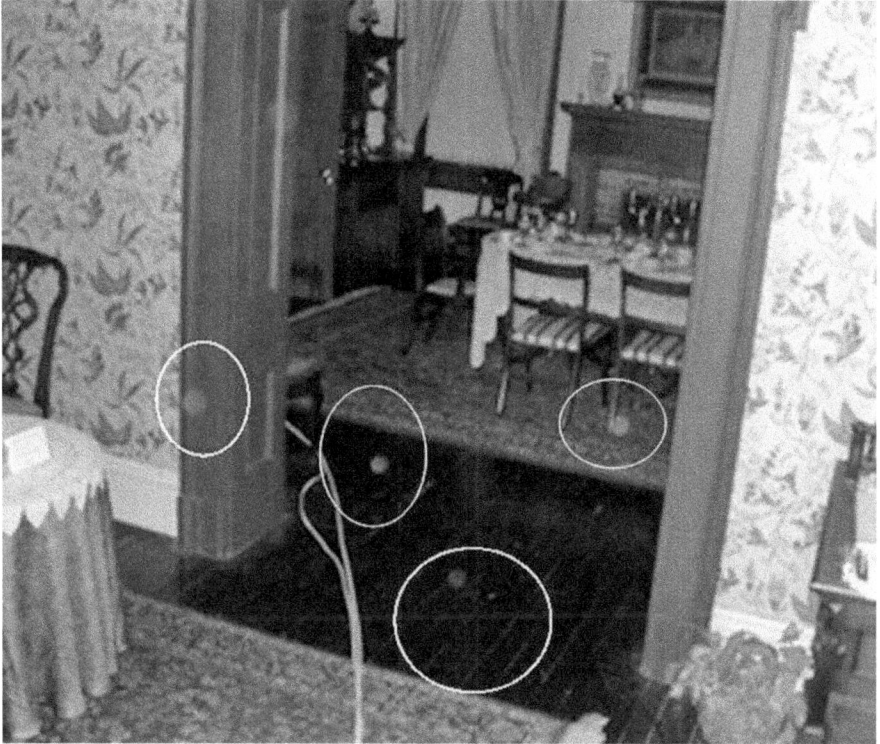

FIGURE 19 DINING ROOM WITH SEVERAL ORBS

FIGURE 20 PORCH ORB

FIGURE 21 PATHWAY WITH MULTIPLE ORBS

FIGURE 22 STAIRS WITH MULTIPLE ORBS CAPTURED ON FILM

Chapter 7

Awareness

Over the years as I would build my psychic abilities and experiences with paranormal investigation, it came to my attention there are a lot of investigators who have a passion for this type of work. Some people are more serious than others. I learned to take care on investigations. Entering abandoned buildings or houses is not a good idea. There is the legal matter of entering abandoned locations as well as the physical safety. Signs saying "KEEP OUT" are there for a reason. Without knowing the purpose and history of the building, it is a risk to enter. Unknown entities could be in residence and without information about which they might be. They could end up creating attachments and following you home.

Some investigators like to work with psychics. Some do not as they depend on their technology to get evidence. When an investigation begins each member of the group has instructions as to what they will want to accomplish.

I usually like to do the psychic work first on an investigation to get the spirits to tell me their story of why they are there. This involves determining emotions, hearing sounds, seeing, and going deep into a meditative state. Sometimes I get visions of spirits or an actual scene, feeling their emotions of fear or depression empathically. It can take several visits to really diagnose the feelings of the spirits, to determine how many there are and what each is all about. There is also psychic hearing. Sometimes I "hear" a spirit talking to my subconscious. During psychic readings, I hear conversations pertaining to the person I am reading for. The words just seem to appear in my mind without being spoken. Meditation always helps me to center and protect myself on cases. Centering is when I balance my energies between earth and heaven. Then I build a protective light around myself. But it also allows me to open myself up to the spirit world to begin communication.

Tech equipment (such as EVP or digital photos) can be matched with psychic findings. I put myself in a state called "Alpha" or "Alpha State". Scientists may call it alpha waves. When I learned meditation is going into Alpha state, I began to explore it. Then with practice, I figured out by closing my eyes, it quiets the conscious mind. Then I realized my subconscious mind really came alive. Being amazed at this outcome, I then realized with practice and study, my psychic abilities come from the subconscious mind. The more I practiced the sharper my abilities became then from before. I would shift my consciousness from everyday mundane thoughts to the world of spirit.

Ghost Hunting

I attended a good number of investigations. Some experiences were more active than others. The one element not discussed very much is the fact there is a lot of waiting. Reality shows and movies make it look like we get activity all the time and we do not. Sometimes paranormal activity can quiet down, especially when there are lots of people on the same case. Sometimes an investigator will try to provoke a spirit which has a high risk to it. I do not recommend provoking spirits, there could be serious consequences. I have highlighted these experiences into segments where it gets right to the moments of actual paranormal activity.

In the year 2012 I started to seek out other paranormal investigators I could work with on a regular basis. The idea of helping people who are being challenged with the paranormal became a focus as well as helping the actual spirits. I started searching the internet and asking people if they knew of any current groups or individuals who were investigating. During the late summer of that year 2012 I was at a Metaphysical store and a psychic reader there gave me a good lead. A month later I met two investigators at the same metaphysical store, and they told me of a meeting. At this meeting I met a few other members of a group and we had a talk about future investigations, and this was the beginning of my ghost hunting career.

North KC Spirits

I am going to start with a case in North Kansas City in an old building that was reopened into a bar and grill. The owner called us to investigate on December 2, 2012. It was cold that night and we could not start until 1am and I thought we are not going to make it, but we did. When I started to get ready to go to the location for the investigation I started to pick up on a female who was saying to me "I know who you are and I know you're coming" and at this moment was when I started to feel a pressure in my chest and a slight tightness in my wind pipe. I got in my car and started to drive to the location and the pressure increased as I drove. I got to the restaurant in North Kansas City which was located behind a drug store. When I parked and got out of my car, I sensed a male spirit was standing on the sidewalk as if he were waiting for me. I had to walk up about a half a block, and he walked ahead of me. Every few seconds he would look back at me as if he were trying to be intimidating. Then I noticed he was wearing a black coat and a black hat that would cover his forehead. He looked something from the 1940's and then he vanished through the door. As I entered the restaurant, I took a good look around and I was wondering why we were in a bar? Paranormal activity can take place anywhere!

In this case I felt the activity was from past of events. We were fronted by a male spirit that which we called "The Mafia Guy" who I believe was the same spirit who introduced himself to me when I arrived. As the night progressed the tightness in my windpipe and the burning feeling in my chest was really starting to increase. There was another team investigating with us. We were all helping to set up the cameras and audio recorders and at the same time this Mafia guy spirit was following me around. I decided not to allow him to affect me. While we were preparing, I started to feel my breathing was becoming difficult and the tightness in my chest kept increasing. I continued to feel this female presence around me then I started to cough hard to the point I could feel my stomach muscles. All these symptoms were increasing, and my breathing was getting more and more difficult. At the same time an emotional downhill began to take place fueled with a sense of fear.

I began to take photos around the location and then we started to do an EVP session with the voice recorders. An EVP is an Electronic Voice Phenomenon, and they record spirit voices that we do not always hear physically. We were asking questions to this Mafia guy and when we played back the recorder, we heard a scruffy male voice that said, "Shut the F*** up" and my jaw dropped to the floor. It seemed he was trying to keep us from asking questions or making sure the other spirit or spirits were not responding to our questions. He sounded very dominating. We discussed the reason why he would wear this black hat over his forehead. The word Tumor came to mind. We think the Tumor could have been the cause of his death.

There was another electronic device we used called the "Tuning Box." It works best for yes and no questions. The green light means yes, and the red light means no. We started to ask if there was a female spirit who was the one affecting my breathing. Her name in life could have been Martha and I think she died from Tuberculosis. This would explain the symptoms I was experiencing. It turns out she was not actually attacking me. She just wanted someone to know what she went through from the TB and wanted to be acknowledged. As I began to sympathize with her all the physical and emotional symptoms began to subside. I finally returned to a normal breathing pattern, I am not sure if it was a type of spirit channeling or emotional bonding. I just knew she wanted to communicate with someone.

I could see her coughing extremely hard and crying while suffering from knowing death was upon her. I had a vision of her in a white night gown with long black hair. Her face was very pale, and she had blood running down the lower part of her face. She would also put her arms around her stomach and lean forward to cough.

FIGURE 23 GHOST IN NKC RESTAURANT

Later in the night we moved over to the south side of the restaurant and we started another EVP session. I felt the male presence continued trying to intimidate us in our investigation. He apparently hated us asking questions. I took a few more photos and just below the flat screen there is an orb I think could be the Mafia guy. The orb is not smooth and may indicate part of the face. To me he looks incredibly angry and wanted us out of there. He also continued to follow me around the restaurant and was breathing down my neck. I felt he wanted to make sure he was in control.

As the investigation was progressing through the night it got to be 3am. Everyone was about to fall asleep. I told everyone the TB symptoms were really subsiding, and I started to feel more relaxed.

This last EVP session we were not getting as much. We started to close around 4:30am and I acknowledged the female spirit one more time and she subsided even more. The next morning Sunday I woke up around 11 and felt extremely exhausted and took the next three days to clear out the emotional residue from the experience.

FIGURE 24 WOMAN WHO TOLD ME HER SYMPTOMS - LIKELY TB
ILLUSTRATION BY KRISTINA MCPHEETERS

Second case 2012 Ghosts of Shawnee Mission

Another case came up in Shawnee Mission, Kansas. A mother and three kids were living in a house where the dish washer was turning on by itself and the kitchen chairs turning over by themselves. This would go on repeatedly and she called for an investigation. The mother said on one occasion when the dish washer turned on and the chairs turned over by themselves, she took her kids out of the house. We never did experience these claims, which I was hoping for. But the mother remained very shaken up.

When all the investigators met up in front of the house the kids left with a relative and the mother stayed for the investigation. Each case begins by letting the spirits know we are not there to hurt them we just want to communicate. The group broke up into smaller groups and walked through different parts of the house with EVP voice recorders. The investigators I was with use psychic readers.

I started to sense a heavy energy in the hallway coming down over my head. I also got the feeling of being watched by a female presence. I sensed there had to be more than one spirit and one was a little girl under the age of eight. The other spirit I saw was of an adult female, who I think was a mother-like figure, but not blood related. A play ball was placed in the center of the living room. We started asking the child spirit to move the ball. I do believe the ball moved just a fraction. I say this because we sat around the ball for quite a long time and it never moved. I think it moved when we started talking to each other. When we stopped talking, we noticed it did move. I think it is the spirit of a little girl. This idea becomes confirmed for me later in the night.

FIGURE 25 ORB IN KITCHEN

An hour or two later, several of us were in the living room with all the lights off and we were asking questions to the spirits. "Can you let us know you are here with us?" The entire ceiling of the living room sounded like a huge explosion. This explosion was so loud I reacted with such amazement and then in seconds we heard a voice sounding like a little girl. But I was not able to make out any specific words. I have never heard a spirit make this loud of a sound. We all felt validated. I do hope to have this kind of experience again. I have heard spirits entering and exiting my home making lighter sounds, but this night was a new experience.

The Haunted Funeral Home

On February 2, 2013, we had a client in Kansas City Kansas at a bar that was a former funeral home. It had an old piano by the back stairs, and we were investigating on the lower level. The cameras were set up by the area where the bodies were cremated, and I got some good photos of activity.

I cannot imagine how many spirits could still be there floating around. While all the equipment was being set up, I stood by where the bodies were cremated and took a good look on the inside and got a creepy feeling. The feeling came from just knowing human corpses were being prepared for actual funeral services at one time. Then I walked over to what looked like a walk-in cooler, which I found out was really for frozen bodies at one time. I stood by there for a few moments. I could feel a pair of eyes on me, I believe to be female. Another investigator also felt he was being watched from the cooler.

We started to work with the EVP recorders later in the night. I noticed a lot of noise coming from the bar upstairs. Which I think hindered the paranormal activity, and it began to quiet down. We were not getting very many responses with our questions. The noise upstairs continued, and it just got quiet for us. The orb photos were about all we got for evidence. I think if it were quieter upstairs, we could have captured more evidence.

We kept the camera recorders going. While I was watching the monitor showing all camera angles, I saw a black shadow pass through one of the cameras. I began to feel we really caught something at this moment. We played it over and over to make sure it was not a shadow from one of the investigators. Recreating the event was the next thing to do. We left all cameras in their same spots and we remained where we were sitting. The one investigator who was walking around made their same route and we saw the same shadow on the monitor from the same camera. Then we knew we had to debunk what we thought was a spirit. Sometimes this can happen, not everything is going to be paranormal. It is a bummer, but it is better to know the truth for the investigators and the client.

FIGURE 26 ORB IN CREMATORIUM

Boonville, Missouri Chapel and House Investigation

FIGURE 27 BOONVILLE HOUSE – BRIGHT ORB NEAR STEPS

The ghost hunting group I was with travelled to Boonville to investigate a pre-Civil War house in 2013. As we were on our way, the group found out about an old Chapel close by. So, we stopped there. It seemed like it was alone, with hardly any repairs done on the structure. I do not think it has been attended in quite some time. The chapel was run down and dusty. But I was able to feel all the activity in this space. There we communicated with children spirits, and there were many of them. From what I remember, I could sense playful energies moving around in various places. I spent most of my time taking photos to catch evidence. Well,

I think I caught a lot of activity. When I saw the phots, there were orbs which could be the children's spirits, especially in the front of the church on the podium. This investigation took about an hour or two. In fact, when I went through the pictures the next day, it seemed like the spirits were starring me through the photos. It was thrilling and eerie at the same time. Then we finished up at the chapel, headed in for our main investigation.

We arrived at our target house in Boonville, MO on a cold night and it was raining on and off. This next client became a friend of the paranormal team. She had a large house I believe was built before the Civil War. She had a day spa business in this house with shiny wooden floors and many rooms. There was also a restaurant with two sections on the lower level.

FIGURE 28 ORB ON WIRES

We set up cameras and voice recorders on three floors. I remember there was one male spirit on the bottom floor. He felt very tall and bigger than life itself. I picked up on him as an energy, but I never actually saw him. However, I could feel his eyes coming down on me. He liked dominating the bottom level in the main bathroom. It seemed also he was trying to intimidate us on our investigation, thinking he could scare us off. To my senses he seems like he was a bigot in life and is still a bigot. I also felt there were many other spirits who were just passing through and had nothing to do with the actual house. The house seemed to serve as an open portal for traveling spirits. But I do believe they were still in their own time and plane, just going about their daily actions.

The overbearing male spirit was giving our client problems in her bedroom of all places and keeping her awake. A person can become vulnerable during the time of sleep. Later in the night we started a sage cleansing with prayers and moved through the house and her bedroom to clear this male spirit out. He was eventually crossed over and he could no longer be a bother to her. I remember the rooms being filled with lots of burning sage. Sage is used to make the spirits leave. It is a powerful herb and appears to work. Even some living people will leave a place filled with burning sage. We did spend the night there in the house. I slept on the upper floor and faced myself to the staircase which included an exceedingly long hallway leading to the staircase. I spent the night watching the hallway to see if anything paranormal would happen during the night. I did sleep, but I kept waking up expecting to see a spirit. I felt them, but I did not see one. I was asked if I wanted to sleep downstairs with the male spirit, but I did not volunteer.

Slave House in Boonville

The group also investigated an old slave house in Boonville. When we were walking up to the house, we noticed that it looked like the house had been there for a long time. It had an old world feeling to it.

FIGURE 29 FACE ABOVE THE DOOR IN THE SLAVE HOUSE

The weather was cold that night. As we all walked into the house, I began to feel an energy that was out of control. Everywhere I went in the house it would follow me. It was right over my head and upper back. I felt I was being bullied by this energy or spirit. As I would walk around the house it stuck with me. When I approached the stairs to the upper levels, it would not follow me up there. It remained on the lower floor. In climbing this staircase, it felt like walking through a tunnel of spirit activity. When I walked back down, spirit on the lower floor was waiting for me, and followed me around again. I decided to take a photo of the front door by the stairs; I captured a green like image of a face at the top of the front door. I feel this was the spirit that had been following me around in the hallway and the living room. It felt as if someone was right on my back. There was also a beaming spirit orb on the bottom, but I do not who it was.

Westport ghost-Winter of 2014

This next case I took on my own in the winter of 2014 in the Westport area of Kansas City, Missouri. I always enjoyed talking to people about paranormal investigations and what I have already experienced. I was talking to a lady at a metaphysical store in the area and she introduced me to a friend of hers who was having experiences in her house that was built in 1914. They both asked me if I could come by and do an investigation in the basement of the house. When I got there, I walked in and saw these old wooden floors and staircase. It felt very warm and grounding.

I started to see that the lady I was doing the investigation for was feeling a slight bit on edge at times and other times she would be very calm. I think the activity was mostly in the basement. I do not think the spirits came to the upper levels very often. I told them I could do a short and simple investigation to start with and see what we were dealing with. I felt it was better to be safe than sorry.

When it came time to head down to the basement, we said a prayer of protection and it a smudge stick of Sage to have with us during the EVP session. We walked down a narrow set of stairs and then down some wooded stairs and then we had to duck our heads down to get all the way down into the basement. It felt very cold and there was a large old-fashioned radio sitting next to the side of the stairs. She would sit at the top of the steps as I would go to the bottom.

When I turned and looked to the right in the far back corner, I noticed a door leading into a room you could not get into. As I looked at the door, I got the feeling I was being watched by something or someone. Then I knew we had our hands full.

I placed the sage stick on a shelf and a voice recorder, and I introduced myself to the spirit or spirits. I told them we are not there to hurt them we just want to talk and see if we can be of help. I decided to get quiet for a while and see what I could pick up on a psychic level. I felt the spirits have been there for a long time. As I got deeper into it, I started to pick up on a male spirit. He seemed very mischievous and even cocky. I saw him with dark hair with a mustache and a slight belly. He liked being in control of situations and people. As I continued, I noticed he was laughing, and I wanted to know why.

A few minutes later I started to pick up on a female spirit. She seemed hesitant and withdrawn. I saw her with blonde hair and a white dress. She even looked a little pale in the face. It felt to me they were both in the room behind the white door we could not get into.

We asked if they would like to talk with us and I gave them permission to talk directly into the voice recorder. I started to take digital photos and what I got in them showed the basement is active. We decided to close the investigation for that day and told the spirits they are not to bother anyone in the house or to follow me home.

On the follow up investigations, we kept on with the EVP sessions and using sage. We always started with a prayer of protection and we would let the spirits know that we just want to talk and see how we can be of help.

This time I used a pendulum for further communication. A pendulum can work in clockwise and counterclockwise directions. The client I was doing the investigation for had a house guest and was on the upper floor in her room meditating. She was in a very peaceful state of mind at the end of her meditation. Suddenly she felt a mischievous feeling taking over. It was also giving her the feeling of dread. This was quite evident to her that this male spirit was in her room and effecting the environment. She described it as a dark male presence.

I confronted this male spirit immediately on his behavior. Why did he feel the need to disturb the house guest with dread during her time of meditation? I do not think he liked me asking him these questions but at the same time he was amused by it all. This is when I started to hear him laughing at us. He thought it was the funniest thing of all to sneak up on people. He kept on laughing so I kept on with questions on his behavior.

Later that night we closed the investigation, and I told the spirits they are to again not to bother anyone in the house and they are not to follow people to other places. Even though I still felt the male spirit was not done with his little pranks. I left the clients house and walked out to my car. I felt the male spirit following me outside and I said to him he is not to follow me home and to stay where he is.

As I was driving home, I noticed the energy in my car changed. I had to really focus on the road. As a prankster spirit, he was influencing my ability to drive. I could still hear his vile laughter. My eyes kept being pulled to the review mirror, as if someone were sitting in the back seat. I pulled into the driveway behind my building and ran up the back stairs. This male spirit was letting me know he was still behind me. I started to unlock the door and it seemed like I could not unlock it fast enough. As I entered through the door, I felt a negative rush behind me. It could almost be described as a fog. I turned quickly towards the back door and I surrounded myself and the doorway with energy, which created a strong protection shield. I told him "No! Go back where you came from." I suddenly slammed the door shut and he was gone within a few seconds. This experience happened so fast. I am grateful to my metaphysical teacher who taught me how to work with these psychic protection methods. Otherwise, no telling what the outcome could have been.

We did one more investigation about a week later and we asked a lot of the same questions from the previous time. When we closed the investigation, he followed me again but only to the outside of the house. I could feel him across the street watching me get in my car. I told him again he was not to follow me home. He seemed a little more subtle this time, maybe he was thinking about his actions.

This case is still open to my knowledge. I thought it was best to bring in additional help. Later the client emailed me and told me her house has been quiet. Since it has been a year since the investigation the spirit has most likely moved on or crossed over. If he did cross over then the female spirit, he was holding there against her will in the basement has

Figure 30 Orb in basement

hopefully also crossed over. I hope to return soon with another team to investigate further.

Overland Park Mansion

This was a short one-time case. I was only there for one night for a follow up. It seems the investigators wanted to further their amount of evidence. Most of the time a follow up is to get more evidence.

The next case I was investigating in overland park Kansas in a very prosperous area. I pulled up to this huge house that looked like a mansion. It was very spacious on the inside as well. The other investigators were already down in the basement. I started to take photos right away. I think we had a good number of people investigating this time. I was only on this case for one night I only have a little to share. But I still enjoyed it.

On the staircase I felt I was being greeted by an actual spirit when I walked in the front door. I took a photo at this precise moment of the staircase. You can see the spirit orb at the top of the steps:

FIGURE 31 ORB BY CHANDELIER

When I entered the basement, I saw an old piano. This photo shows spirit orbs surrounding the piano which looked like an antique to me. The thing about Antiques is they can come with their own spirits. A spirit or spirits can be attached to items they were attached to in life. I believe when you bring Antiques into your home there is the risk of a spirit coming home with you. The spirit orbs in the photo around the piano could have come with it or they were already there.

I made my way back to the living room and sat on the staircase and focused on what was greeting me when I walked in earlier. Then I started talking with another investigator about my past with the paranormal. Just within minutes I felt like someone was playing with my right ear. It felt like a child was trying to get my attention. I could feel the small fingers touching my ear very gently. This occurred during a conversation with the other investigator. Then I began to pay attention to this experience, and I decided to let this child be playful. I feel it was a little boy playing around on the staircase and on the upper floor. I am not sure who this little boy was, and I do not believe there were any further discussions.

The upstairs photo of the hallway was like walking through a tunnel of activity. I felt this is where the child spirit spent most of his time. I located myself at the top of the stairs during an EVP session. I could feel many spirits moving around in the hallway. I think some of them were just passing through, but I do believe the child spirit made this hallway as a main area to make himself known. For the most part I feel this house is highly active.

Parkville Ghost

In the spring of 2013, I was on another case in Parkville MO. I thought it was a little strange to be investigating an apartment. It had one bedroom and a rather good size living room. When I got there just a few people were investigating. I headed into the bedroom and I noticed the center had a huge amount of pressure coming down on my head. Then I turned to the closet and the doors were pulled open and I stood in the middle and I picked up on a female spirit. She had her hands well gripped on the bar holding hangers. It seemed to be a hiding place for her hoping no one would know she was there. I also picked up on her facial features. Like most of the bones were broken. She also had on layers of makeup, especially on her lips. It looked like a shade of red. Her eyes were bulging outward because of her bones being broken. She seemed very scared when I was standing in front of the closet. Another male investigator came in the room and she became even more unnerved.

I told another investigator what I saw and felt in the bedroom then I walked out into the living room. I sat down and we compared notes with another investigator. Someone else saw a black orb moving in the front room. What I saw in my vision was her facial features looked very beaten. As I looked more carefully at it her facial bones looked badly crushed. I feel an unexpected motion throwing her forward causing the deformation of her facial bones. The cheek bones were crushed inward and the nose and jaw line. This could have caused her life to suddenly end abruptly. I believe she was still there because she was not ready to cross over. She might have had a connection with this apartment.

While I was walking through the living room, I started to admire a chime sitting on a lamp post. As I stood in front of it, I felt very compelled to ring it. I rang the chime and it put out a high pitch sound. It made the room feel peaceful. My mind was saying it will become significant during the investigation. I think this female spirit admired this chime. She could be the reason why I felt so compelled to ring it.

FIGURE 32 GHOST LADY WITH A CRUSHED FACE HIDING IN THE CLOSET
ILLUSTRATION BY ADAM TILLERY

Then everyone moved into the bedroom to begin the investigation. Since it was where most of the activity was occurring. We turned off the lights and started to ask questions with the Tuning Box. We first asked her to let us know of her presence. Then a moment later we heard the chime in the living room ring, and we knew no one else was in the apartment with us. We felt excited of this experience. The words I said was "Did you hear that?" this was her way of confirming she was there with us. These moments are incredibly special when we have these kinds of experiences and I hope to have more of them.

This female spirit was not responding to the questions like we hoped. She seemed to be holding back for a certain reason. Since we were talking with a female spirit, we decided to have the two female investigators stay in the room and let us two male investigators wait outside. The females were able to get her to calm down and talk with them.

A short while later the females said it was ok to come back into the bedroom. We asked her how she died, and we were getting an answer of a possible beating and this could explain some of the facial features in my vision of her in the bedroom closet. With further discussion with the tuning box we discovered she was in a car wreck and she used to live in the same apartment building as our client. I think this can explain why our clients make up items started to mysteriously disappear. Then days later it would reappear out of nowhere. I was hoping the chime in the front room would ring for us again, but it never did.

Lee's Summit Spirit

On April 5, 2014, I was invited to a case in Lee's Summit, Missouri to help a lady client who was confronted by a negative spirit which felt threatening to her. I prepared my-self for this investigation by grounding and building a bubble of light around myself and asking my spirit guides for protection. On this case I put sea salt in my shoes to ground myself. Sea salt is known to be protective and grounding. I was taking no chances.

When I arrived at the location of the house I walked up to the front door and I was greeted by a Siberian husky and he was very social with us. I let the team know I was there and then I headed upstairs. While the cameras were being set up, I started to pick on a male spirit. The feeling was very heavy, and I could feel those sensations in my chest. I walked by the main bedroom and felt this could be the cen-ter of activity. Then I walked through this hallway to these other rooms and to my left was where I began to feel the eyes of this male entity on me. I got a little bit of a chill, but I showed him no fear. I felt this room on my left was where he liked to hide out and the room that was further back and had no doorway to it was another hiding place.

I headed back downstairs and sat down and interviewed our client. I asked her what her first experience was.

She said she was in her kitchen preparing food and she picked up a sharp knife, and at that moment a male voice told her to stab herself in the throat. Her reply was "I can't, I have people who rely on me." She began to pray for help and placed the knife in the sink and left the kitchen.

That same night she was awakened and felt a heavy dark-ness holding her down. This dark entity had no face and she could only turn her head but could not move the rest of her body. As she was being held down by this dark force with no face she began to pray again for help. At that very moment, the heaviness was gone. Then she called one of the investi-gators and explained what happened. This investigator told her to wear a cross and start smudging her house with Sage. Dark spirits do not like Sage, and it can cause paranormal activity to quiet down. Then she began to read Psalms 23 in the Bible. Then she felt it was important to check up on her other family members to make sure everyone was all right.

The next night she was awakened again. but this time it was not as bad as the night before. This was a brief encounter with the same negative force who seemed to notice her sacred gear such as the cross, the Bible, and the sage. These sacred tools can be used to drive off activity or at least quiet things down for a while. I told her what I was picking up on earlier and that this entity likes to hide out in the room next to her bedroom.

She keeps the Bible open to Psalm 23 for security of the dark energy. She also continues to wear her cross and uses sage when she needs to. We started to use the tuning box and the EVP recorders to ask questions. The first question is usually asked first such as "Are you here with us" or "Give us a sign that you are here". One of the investigators began to ask "How old are you" different age numbers were suggested, and we found that we were talking with two little girls under the age of ten. They were responding rather good as they also seemed distracted. There would be no response on the tuning box at times.

Questions to the two little girl spirits:

"Is there someone else with you?

Girl spirits "Yes"

"Is it a male?

Girl spirits "Yes"

"Does he bother you?"

Girl spirits "Yes"

"Is he trying to keep you from answering our questions?

Girl spirits "Yes"

"Does he scare you?

Girl spirits "Yes"

"Is it the man that scared to lady who lives in this house?

Girl spirits "YES"

"Is he in the room with us now?

Girl spirits "No response"

"Is he in the room with us now? We got no response.

Then we heard banging sounds on the wall to the next room. My eyes came wide open and at that very moment one of the investigators decided to go in the next room alone to talk with this male spirit who we think was banging on the wall, but I don't think any communication was received. I think he was continuing to distract the two girls from talking with us. I continued to feel the eyes on me and the dark feeling in my chest got heavier.

I had an updated interview with our client a couple of months later. She followed up on the seven-day cleanse with candles and holy water while saying Psalm 23. Then she did it for another seven days and seemed to have made her home much calmer for a while. But then the activity started to pick up with her sons' girlfriend.

The girlfriend was taking a shower and started to get the feeling of being watched. As this feeling increased, she felt hands on her back pushing her forward, but no one was there. The next day she was pushed again in the shower and felt the same hands her back. Then her son was pushed in the shower as well. They all knew this male entity was still in the house. Another experience with our client happened when she was sleeping and felt hands under her blankets and pulling her feet to the end of the bed. This was startling to her and then felt the hands again pulling her feet to the end of the bed. She still had her sacred gear with her and one of those items was the Bible. Which she always kept open to Psalm 23 and would start reading it. She kept on wearing her cross as another sacred tool.

Our client would take pictures and then she started to take pictures of mirrors and they would show apparitions. One photo she told me of was an apparition of a man in a period suit walking with a cane and had a long beard looking right at her. That really got my attention, and I became interested in taking pictures of mirrors after that.

I later learned that this male entity has been active at her mother's house for years and followed her to her own house in Lee's Summit. The entity was moving through a portal between the two places. It all started when she was young, and this portal was opened with a Ouija board. That activity invited the male entity to enter the lives of her family. They were in the basement and they most likely thought it would be a fun game. I would not tell people to rule out Ouija boards, just that they must learn how to work with the board correctly. When we entered the basement of her childhood house it had a smell of death like something died down there. We got all cameras set up and started to do an EVP session in the basement with this foul stench.

During the EVP session it seemed to me that this male entity wanted to cross over since we were offering to help him with the process. Meanwhile I was upstairs attending the monitor for all cameras. I was able to see orbs moving around with certain directions. I was alone on the upper floor for about twenty minutes. I could hear different tapping sounds around the house while the wind was blowing intensely outside.

Then we all gathered in the basement for the crossing over ceremony. That is to help a spirit move on to the light. I felt this male spirit responding to the prayers during the ceremony by the investigators. It was set with two lines of candles creating a lane. This lane allowed the spirit to move through to cross over. It is like the idea of an airplane gaining speed for flight. I immediately could tell the energy change and the foul smell of death was gone--like a dark cloud was lifted off the house. It was lighter and smelled fresh. I no longer felt this male entity. This was a successful crossing over ceremony.

This was an amazing experience that I hope to have again.

Fort Osage Ghosts

FIGURE 33 FORT OSAGE PHOTO: MARGIE KAY 2018

In the fall of 2013, we headed out to Sibley, Missouri to investigate Fort Osage, a historical site that was originally built in 1808 and was used for a trading post. Soldiers were housed there to protect the area and as well as the trading post. They also had good relations with the Osage Indians and Missourian settlers. The fort also sits in view of the Missouri river. I really enjoyed this case because I got to lead groups through the different sections of the fort during a paranormal investigation that was open to the public. More people showed up than I ever imagined, and it was very cold that night.

The first visit at the fort was like walking into a piece of history. Looking around the place and taking photos I saw it was in particularly good shape. All of the investigators were given a kind welcome as equipment was being set up. There was a lot to cover with the cameras. When darkness came it became very dark there. Everyone had flashlights and started taking photos. This investigation was just a regular night for us.

On the second visit at the fort was the public investigation with all investigators leading different groups through the various sections. I think I had about three different groups that were in good numbers. I had my flashlight and an EVP recorder. There are four Bunkhouses and at each corner of the fort and they all have cannons on the top floor. I had people sit on the bottom floor and turned all the lights out. I would start off by asking questions. I like to start with "Are there any spirits here with us?" Sometimes it would be noticeably quiet. Spirits were communicating with us this night.

With the second group I took through the fort we got to the third Bunkhouse and turned all lights out and we sat on the bottom floor. I started to ask questions first and I felt we had a male spirit wanting to respond to us on the top floor. There were footsteps sounding like a soldier. We could hear him walking around above. I asked him to hit the wall for us. A sudden loud hit we heard. Then I asked him to do it again and we got an even louder hit. I told him thank you and asked him to repeat the sound. We got a third hit and a fourth hit. People were excited and it seemed to me some of them were ready to jump out of their skin. Then at the end of the EVP session everyone ran up the stairs to take pictures. As I walked around the top floor, I had a few people tell me they got touched. One of them was a guy who told me he got grabbed on the leg. But I think the visitors were really enjoying the activity and sharing photos with each other.

I am incredibly pleased how these photos turned out. I was not even sure if I was catching paranormal activity. What is always interesting to see is I can take a high number of pictures and have nothing show up. Then suddenly a single photo is showing spirits could be present which takes time and patience.

FORT OSAGE LOWER BLOCKHOUSE AREA ORB

FIGURE 34 ORB IN BUNKHOUSE

Sugar Creek Ghosts

This next case was much more than what I was expecting. Of course, I had to wait over forty days before I could document this experience. The reason is to disconnect myself on every level from these spirits so they would have no effect on me any further. On the way in the car I was clearing my mind and asking for protection. At the same time, I picked up on a young male spirit who seemed he was in his late teens and was a little mischievous. Then a minute later I picked on another spirit who was a native Indian woman. She stepped out in front of the male spirit like she was protecting me from him or from something else. When I got to the location of the case it was an old gymnasium built in the late 40's or early 50's. It had no air conditioning.

Before I walked up to the building, I was checking the batteries in my digital camera and it was working perfectly fine. I was ready to start the investigation. Five minutes after I walked into the building, I felt a burning feeling on my left calf muscle. I thought this was very strange. A few minutes later it started to sting, and a red mark appeared. I am not sure if I scraped my leg up against something or if this was a scratch from a spirit. I started to show this red mark to the other investigators, and we think it was a possibility a spirit scratched me. Then I thought why? Then suddenly my camera broke for no reason. This could have been the same spirit. I ended up using my phone camera for the evening.

Another investigator and I decided to head to the lower level and use a digital tuning box. We also set up an EVP recorder with the tuning box and took lots of pictures. While asking questions I started to ask if there was a young male spirit and we got a yes from the tuning box as it lit up. I asked him questions concerning his life. I asked him if he was in his late teens and if he was involved with activities in the gymnasium. According to the tuning box he was there in the 1980's and he really had no interest in attending sports. He also seemed very shy about personal questions. Then I asked if there was a native Indian woman with us and the tuning box lit up again for yes and she was there with others from her tribe. Then I asked the male spirit if he was the one who scratched me earlier in the evening. I kept getting the answer Yes, but I do not think he is the one who did it. I suspected it was another male spirit I picked up on that was trying to stay hidden from me. He seemed dirty and very rugged looking with a mustache. I don't' think he was a clean person. He had bad breath and was not very pleasant. I started to have a suspicion this dead guy and I had a past life together not ending well.

After some time, we decided to head back up to the main floor of the gym. I took a short break and talked with the client. This person told me one of his family's own experiences of heading to the lower level and had a large door slammed shut on them directly. They also have seen other spirits in the gym on the main floor. As we were talking, I was still concentrating on the scratch on my leg. The stinging feeling continued to increase. We eventually closed the case for the night. *Why?*

A few days later I made a phone call to a person who is also an intuitive and an investigator. I told her I thought it was a male spirit who had scratched me. Further background information revealed he was a male spirit who I had a past life with in the 1880's. I was the sheriff in the area and I was hunting down a criminal who was hiding out. As the sheriff, I shot and killed this male criminal and his spirit never left the area. He must have remembered me when I got there for the paranormal investigation. This seems to make sense to me because when I spoke with another investigator about one of the EVP recordings. A male spirit voice was heard saying my name Devin and I was to be hit in the face. Then it repeated. At this moment I decided to not go back on the case for my own safety.

The Dream Sequence

A week later I had a dream sequence where I was back at the gymnasium alone trying to get back into the building. As I observed the premises, I noticed the weather began to turn very dark and windy. The windows of the building became dark as well. I started to walk up to the main doors. Suddenly the native Indian woman stood in front of me and prevented me from entering the building. The weather got even darker. It seemed like the native Indian woman was surrounding the building with an energetic force preventing me form going in and to never return if I want to feel safe. When I awakened from the dream, I felt strongly it was a warning not to go back on the case.

In August of 2015 I attended the paranormal conference over a hot weekend. There was no air conditioning in the building. I did have an interesting experience with the children spirits. I had a booth there with my friend. We had to move from the lower floor to the upper level. I had to go back down to make sure that we got everything moved. At the bottom of the stairs I heard the shuffling noises. I figured it had to be feet of small children. They were being very playful, and I heard them with my own ears.

It felt like they were running little circles around me with their feet hitting the floor. I think they were trying to get my attention and they got it. They were trying to amuse each other. I do not think they were trying to scare anyone; they were just being children. It felt like a burst of energy was moving around me and it was so sudden. It was very noticeable I could only feel their presence around my legs and not any higher.

I began to wonder what game they were playing that would involve that would involve the sound of running feet. It could have been a chase game or maybe Ring around the Rosie which is based off an old folksong about the plague. As I continued to notice these children on the lower level, I picked up on them getting back up into the gym area. I started listening to the next speaker and I was giving this person my full attention. But my attention was being pulled away from a feeling of being watched. It started with a single set of eyes then two then three and it built from there. I began to wonder if I needed to be concerned. As I tuned in more it did not have a threatening feeling. Then I picked up on child like laughter and I figured it had to be the children from a few moments ago. They just continued to play their games and just be children.

Downtown ghost

In the summer of 2014 in the downtown area of Kansas City I was on a case that had a lot of activity. The client living in this loft was surrounded with spirits. She left and did not return for the next two weeks.

The occupant asked investigators for help. During the investigation I felt this rush of air moving right through and around me. My entire being felt like it was floating. For a few moments I felt a charge was running from my head down through my arms and legs. A rush of wind came over me even though there was no wind blowing through the hallway. It felt slightly cold but not overbearingly cold. I was in awe from this experience and told another investigator that a spirit just moved right through me. There were too many people on this particular investigation, and they seemed to disrupt the spirit energy.

Chapter 8

Solitary Investigations

House Walk and the Watcher--Raytown MO

Summer of 2016 was extremely hot and humid. Kansas City had a long heat wave and I was getting through it the best I could. As I continued with my Reiki practice, I kept meeting new people who also have a Reiki practice. I believe it has enhanced my psychic abilities to communicate with other energies or spirits. Reiki is mainly about healing the soul.

One day another healer and I started to talk about spiritual issues and what we have experienced with the paranormal. As I got to know her more, she and I began to have a higher level of trust. She became a client for me to do a reading on her house. She had been having uncomfortable occurrences for a good number of years. While I was preparing myself to investigate it seemed her house began to talk to me in my head. Something or someone there knew I was coming to do a reading on the location...that was not living.

The day came for me do the reading and I pulled up to her house and walked up to the door. The lady I was there for invited me in and the first thing I got was a huge wave of heavy somewhat dark clouds of energy. It took over the entire front room and I was unable to move. It had many layers to it. I stood in the one spot for a good amount of time. Very slowly I began to move about the house in the main hallway. The first room we entered was a room used for healing work. This space had a lot of good energy because it was also a haven for the client. Music was also performed in this room. She told me she played the Cello.

I continued down the hallway into a room that was all blue, almost like a sky blue. As I observed this room, I started to get a pull towards the closet which did not have any doors on it. It might have had sliding doors on it at one time. Next to the closet is a window with a white curtain. In the space between the closet and the window, I got a sense of a doorway or portal to the spirit world. I told the client a male spirit routinely comes into this blue room through the portal and watches the person who once occupied this space.

While I was in the blue room, I spent some time observing the portal. I felt it had been there for an awfully long time, and possibly before the house was built there. Then I walked into the master bedroom. The more time I spent in there I started to figure out that room was also active.

As I moved between bedrooms and the living room I picked up on completely different vibrations. I do not feel the male spirit had any interest in other parts of the house except the bedrooms. I started to investigate the blue room again and I noticed the male spirit was there but not in the same room. I walked back into the master room and I was pulled to the corner closest to the mattress. Suddenly, I realized he was standing in the corner I was pulled to.

This is when I got a good look at this male entity. He was very tall with thin grey scraggly hair. He was extremely thin and had on clothes that looked dirty and worn out. I think he did a lot of physical labor in life. He had on a button shirt showing his chest. I could see how he really was from seeing the bones in his chest. I saw he had long arms and fingers. His legs were also exceptionally long. When I saw his face the cheek bones were large, and his mouth looked like they were being sucked inward. He also had a large jaw line and chin and a long nose.

As I observed the spirit in the corner, I told the lady client he stands in that room in the corner closest to the mattress he watches people as they sleep. I sensed that he came in through the portal from the blue room. But I do not think he has anything to do with the family or the house. He comes and goes as he pleases through the portal. I do not think the spirit does a lot except watch people.

My client sent me a phone text and told me her daughter used to sleep in the back room when she was young. The daughter told her mother she would feel someone watching her. She would wake up in the middle of the night and see a bright blue ball at the end of her bed and it would sit there for a while. My client said that was the first time she ever heard her daughter tell her those details. Sometimes people are not always ready to reveal information of their paranormal experiences. They did put white salt around the house and all the rooms. The house did feel better after that. I believe that was just the beginning of the healing process.

We had a follow up on the phone and my client told me she went down into her basement. Something down there gave her the creeps. She said she felt watched and a little threatened.

I walked back into the living room and it seemed like walking into a black mist. Most of the darkness was all emotional and this person was still living. I told the female client most of the dark energy was coming from a male. A lot of issues have never been seriously taken care of professionally. I told her it felt layered and suppressed. I sensed he would spend good amounts of time sitting in the living room. I believe he is feeding this black mist that felt somewhat like an actual entity.

As I continued the reading, I noticed this black mist was getting thicker and it was moving in a circular motion throughout the room. I feel if the husband does not take care of his emotional state this black mist could take over the living room entirely. One other detail I picked up on was this chair close to the front door. I had a vision of him coming home in work clothes and sitting in this chair. During this time, he becomes quiet and feeds this black mist. But he is not aware of it. Surely enough he came home and sat in the exact chair by the front door in his work clothes.

A short while later I moved back into the bedrooms to see what more I could get on this male spirit. I do not think he is going to do much of anything except watch people sleep. Kind of like a creeper who is trying to stay anonymous. After the daughter moved out on her own this male spirit no longer had an easy target to spy on. He moved to next person who would be easy to creep around. That person was my client's husband.

The next follow up was December 3, 2016 Saturday evening. This was the third investigation, and I had a second person with me this time. We had additional equipment such as EMF detectors. These units pick up on energy in the environment. They will light up when spirits get close to them. We did a complete light out investigation. On our way to the clients home we were having a conversation and I started go into a meditative state and the spirits started talking to me. They knew we were coming there to investigate. I felt a little bit of resistance from one of them. I was getting a sense of two spirits and it was important we investigate the basement. Spirits can communicate with you in advance when you plan to investigate a location. I was wondering if the man spirit in the master room was going to communicate one more time. I had a feeling he was going to. We ended up taking a wrong turn instead of listening to the GPS delaying our arrival time. I do not think it was a coincidence at all.

We finally arrived and I introduced investigator number 2 to our client. I did notice a huge improvement in the living room. It felt much lighter. A lot of emotional healing has taken place. From my first visit the living room was very heavy and it felt like all the emotional turmoil was turning into an entity of its own. I do think most of it goes back to childhood.

We turned out all the lights in the back of the house to start the investigation. The blue room was the first and we started to introduce ourselves to the spirits. I had the EVP (voice recorder) going the entire time. The EMF detectors began to light. When it is three lights an energy is getting close. When it is five a spirit could be right by you. That is a good time to put your hand out and feel if there is a cold spot near you. It seemed to me this spirit moved to the master room. We moved in there and activity kicked up. It seemed to me the man spirit who watches people sleep was in there with us. I asked him what his name was, and I got the letter "P". Then the name Phillip came to mind. I asked the man watcher if his name was Phillip. Both EMF detectors started really lighting up. Another unit with colored lights going in a circle was lighting up on the right side. Then I picked up on an energy shift and it was the man watcher moving to the opposite side of the master room. I had my other investigator move the circled light unit to the opposite side. I told the spirit watcher I knew he was trying to avoid us. The circled lights started to light on the left side this time. We asked him if he was watching our client's daughter when she was living there in the blue room. The EMF detectors started to light up to about three lights. To us that meant "YES" he was watching the daughter. But we think the man still watches the husband sleep.

After a while we had to move down to the basement. Our client took us through the garage and opened a door. The staircase was very steep. At this moment I knew there was something down there waiting for us. As we walked down this steep staircase our client turned off the light and closed the door. The only light in the room was from our phones. We began to set up for another EVP session. We also had the laser light to catch moving shadows. After a good five to ten minutes the energy began to change, and I started to feel different. It seemed I was being pulled into a deep trance state. I remained standing and I started to pick up on a male Indian spirit. He was making me fully aware of his presence. In my mind I could see an image of a male Indian with long black hair. A few minutes later he jumped inside my body and started to tell me his story. This experience did not make me feel ill. It was very subtle.

The visions I got seemed extremely huge. The next thing in the vision was a bonfire bigger than life. The energy of it felt incredibly positive as if it was a celebration. Its flame was enormously powerful, and I had to look up to see the top of it. I started to feel a circular motion taking place almost like a ritual. I noticed it was going clockwise with chanting. Then the male Indian began to tell me it was him and his family around the bonfire celebrating and giving thanks. I began to feel a bit of warmth from the bonfire, and it seemed like I was taken back in time as a witness.

I finally came out of the channeling state and became aware of my surroundings again. Then I remembered I had another investigator with me as well. He was managing the tech equipment and putting the laser light in different places. I had him place it on the floor in the middle of the room. Then the male Indian spirit began to communicate with me again. I picked up on the second part of his name and I asked him if it was "Eagle"? The Periscope began to light up in a circular motion. Then I asked him if he was missing his family around the bonfire. Then Periscope began to light up again in a circular motion. It remained lit as I asked him if he was waiting for his family to return by keeping himself on our client's property. My next question was "Would you like to cross over to the light"? The Periscope went out completely. I took that as a "NO". We gave it a few more minutes and moved upstairs to the living room.

Our client and her husband were ready to do the final EVP session with us and we turned out all lights in the entire house. I told them this was a good time to ask questions they might have for the spirits. We placed the Periscope in the center of the living room and started to work with the EMF detectors all at the same time. I told our client I got the name "Phillip" from the male watcher spirit in the back bedrooms. I still feel he was waiting for his family to return. Otherwise, I have no idea why he is there in her house. We turned off all the lights and started the final EVP session for the night.

A vision occurred during the time of this final EVP session with our clients attending. The first question was to the spirit Phillip. We asked a good number of questions but got no response. I think the Indian spirit started to communicate with us. In this vision I saw him coming up through the floor from the waistline up. I knew it was him because I could see his black hair and arms. As we finished the questions he disappeared back down through the floor and all communication ended.

About a week or two later our female client sent a message about a voice she heard in the hallway of her house. It had to of startled her when this male voice out of nowhere said "She needs to be dead". When I saw this message, I was startled as well. As we talked about this experience, she began to have calmness in her voice. She mentioned her mother being extremely ill. The Indian spirit who I think is the one was talking to her. I do not think he meant to scare her. But I do think he was talking about her mother's wellbeing.

My conclusion after three investigations I do not think there is anything dangerous. They might feel a little unsettled at times. I think making peace with these two spirits can help to make the environment more comfortable.

A few months later, they decided the house was becoming more difficult to take care of. Their expenses began to pile up. Once our clients decided to put their house up for sale, the spirits began to respond by holding on to them. From what I was told it sounds like an emotional hold. I think it is coming from the Indian spirit mostly. The old man spirit in the bedroom is not quite as concerned, he just wants someone to watch. The Indian spirit has grown quite attached to the husband and the wife. I began to wonder if a bond or relationship has taken place. The Indian spirit is not happy about them leaving the house for good. I do believe spirits can put a hold on someone if they do not want them to leave.

I had another talk with our client in January of 2018; she was telling me one of the main obstacles she just discovered with selling their house. Her husband admitted to her that he was going over to their house at night after work and sitting in the basement, trying to communicate with the spirits and taking pictures with his cell phone. Unfortunately, the spirits still had a hold on him on an emotional level. She said to him "This is the reason our house is not selling. You have to stop." He finally told the spirits he can no longer be there and decided to cut off all attachments. The next day their house sold.

What kind of new owners would be living in the house? Are the spirits ready for the change? I also began to wonder if the new owners will even know these two spirits are in the house. They may or may not believe in the spirit world. Our clients found a town house to live in the opposite side of the city.

Belvoir Winery, Liberty MO 2016

FIGURE 35 BELVOIR WINERY

In September of 2016 I made my first visit to the Belvoir Winery in Liberty MO. This site is well-known for being extremely haunted. After thirty minutes of driving, I came upon this enormous location. It contained a good number of buildings. This first visit was an event put on by a famous psychic who I have seen on paranormal reality shows. The main building has been completely renovated into full function. While walking through I was taken by the view. Then I noticed a huge crowd came to hear this famous psychic. At the end of the night's event, I learned they have ghost hunts in the other buildings on the property.

I returned on November 18th of 2016. The paranormal investigation group was getting ready to start. While we were waiting in the main building, I was getting ready to sit at one of the tables. Before I sat down, I felt someone blowing at my forehead. But I was the only one standing. This had to be a mischievous spirit. They divided thirty people into four different groups. I was in group one and we started with the morgue on the bottom of the hospital. It was extremely cold through the night and very windy. We walked down into the lower entrance of the hospital. As you can see from in the pictures the buildings being investigated are in disrepair.

As we continued to investigate in the Morgue, I had an EVP voice recorder going to the entire time. It was also pitch black down there in the morgue without flashlights. On one of the tables there was a flashlight, but I had no idea it was there. It suddenly turned on by itself and I turned around very quickly and became extremely impressed. The guide we had was asking if the spirit was female. I heard him ask is this Mae James. Then he asked her if she wanted to talk with the flashlight. This is when I heard a voice on my own EVP that said YES. It sounded like a female voice. Research showed her full name was Emma Mae McGinley, grandniece of Jesse James. Her grandmother was named Fanny and she was the half-sister of Jesse James.

It was also said during the investigation Emma Mae supposedly died in the morgue we were standing in. The flashlight kept turning on and off with yes and no questions. Another EVP voice I got on a playback, what is your name was the next question. I got a voice saying "James" this was exciting, and I got a chill going up my arms and back. This voice did sound a like a male voice. Those are always the moments that are cherished in paranormal investigations.

Then we moved to the upper levels of the hospital. I saw a statement spray painted on the wall. "Do not go in there" well, we were all over the place. A cross was also spray painted on the wall. It was getting colder and the wind kept blowing doors around and scaring people. We also got a lot of flashlight action on the upper floor. The group leader would play different types of music and would ask the spirit to turn on the flashlight if they liked the music. Big band music seemed the most effective.

I really like the outdoor photos I got showing spirit orbs. To me that shows there are spirits inside and outside of the buildings. I would not be surprised if there are human spirits walking around the grounds. When I took photographs, I got the feeling of being watched by more than one set of eyes. I quietly walked out on my own for a moment to get these shots. It is not always safe to walk away from the group.

The next building was the old folk's home. I felt like I was being watched by a lot of different spirits. It was almost like we were intruding on many different people. The energy felt much heavier and darker in this building. The conditions were a lot worse with the double staircase all crashed in. The wind was also blowing through here as well. I was getting so cold by this time my legs were freezing. There was almost a full moon shining in and lighting up one of the rooms. I felt very blessed by the moon as if it were lighting up our path.

The energy got heavier for me as we continued through the old folk's home. In these photos you can see many spirit orbs in green and blue. Some of them are glowing and travel in pairs.

In this part of the walk I picked up on various emotions. They were not all positive. There was an energy there I felt was extremely negative. I do not believe this location has anything demonic there. But I do believe people will expect to see a demon that is not there.

When our guide took the group to one of the upper floors it seemed this negative energy was increasing. I began to experience heaviness on my head and shoulders. Something in there wanted me to feel dread. As we walked through the dark cold windy hallways it seemed there were these small entities above us attaching themselves to the ceiling and the walls. They were moving around like spiders. Some people might call them demonic. I would call them little "energy drainers". I could feel their eyes staring down at us. It would not surprise me if other people were feeling heaviness or dread. These entities I think we are trying to feed off the living.

I do not think they just came there to the location. My senses tell me they were created by humans. The winery has been heavily investigated over the years. Thought forms are more powerful than people think. The mental expectation of a demon/evil has created this negative energy. I believe if people stop with the demon hunt, the energy could change. This means putting in positive thought forms. I never even thought of looking for a demon at the winery.

The vision I got of these energy draining creatures were black oval shaped bodies with two legs on each side. They had a set of wide eyes with very sharp vision. These nasty creatures were all around us looking down at the visitors. Their legs would stick to the walls and the ceiling. This vision continued the rest of the time we were in the building. I also saw they were following us through the tour of the building until we left. Once we got outside the pressure and dread were gone.

FIGURE 36 BLACK ENERGY DRAINERS IN THE SHAPE OF BUGS

The last thing I got on the way out was a vision of an old man in a wheelchair. He was acknowledging me and communicating to me telepathically. He did not have a happy life. I got the impression he did not want to move on, and he wanted to stay in the physical realm. Sometimes spirits have unfinished business and can remain attached to a building. This experience happened so quickly; he was there then he was gone.

We were not able to enter all the buildings. I think a couple of them are going to be torn down. But besides that, I believe every building on the property is active with spirits. When you investigate the Winery, you need to prepare yourself because this location is said to be one of the most haunted places in the United States.

FIGURE 37 WINERY HALLWAY CROWDED WITH MULTIPLE ORBS

I do not support the idea of provoking spirits in any way. You are just asking for trouble. It is best to enter the buildings with the highest respect for the spirits who reside there.

This building was extremely cold, and the wind was blowing through the windows. Occasionally it seemed doors were being blown around and slammed shut, which made people jump at times. I do recall having the feeling of being watched by many sets of eyes. I think some of the spirits are wondering why living people keep coming back to investigate. It seems to me some of them just want to rest. I also wonder if any of them want to cross over or need help crossing over. Our guide told us a few of the buildings are in the plans to be renovated which might wake up more paranormal activity even if they have been asleep for a long time.

Tornado hit

August 25th Friday night 2017 2nd investigation

As fall of 2017 began to approach I started to focus on a return to the Winery, to follow up on my findings. The weather was perfect this time around. It was cool with a clear sky and a Waxing moon almost half full. It had a different feeling to the place arriving there with the sun still shining. I was also thinking about how I was going to rediscover my findings from the year the before. Was I going to have any similar experiences?

As the day was approaching it seemed to me the souls still existing at the winery were saying "We know you are coming," which happens quite often. Thirty people divided up into four different groups. The group I was with started in the Old Folks Home. I was wondering if the buildings were going to be hot, but the temperature was perfect. This first part of the investigation was noticeably quiet at first. It began to pick up with a few EVPs. (A digital recorder to pick up spirits voices) I was taking lots of digital photos. A digital camera can pick up what the human eyes cannot always see.

It finally got dark outside by 8:30 pm and the building became completely black. I started to walk down a long hallway with a few other people. I got the feeling we were being watched. I sensed something more was about to happen!

As I gazed my eyesight straight ahead, I noticed someone was looking at me. A head peeked out from the side of the hallway. Then it pulled back, and few seconds later I saw a shadow human figure walk across the hallway, from the left side to the right side. I yelled out on what I just saw, and three other people came over by me, hoping to see this figure. Suddenly a cold feeling began to surround the group. It seemed this shadow figure was making its presence known to us. I felt this energy come towards us and move above us as it began to surround the group. It got cold for a moment, and this coldness surrounded the group. It seemed this coldness began to climb on a guy in the group. He said he felt it on his back and shoulders. This experience occurred for about two or three minutes. But it was exciting at the same time.

When we told our guide, he did not seem surprised at all. When I told him exactly what happened he told us shadow figures are often seen in the old folk's home, they will peek out of the walls or walk in the hallways. It was an awesome experience.

The next building was the nursing home. We had to walk further back on a trail through some trees and it was pitch black outside. The moon was still looking amazing and lighting our way in its waxing mode. The group leader was shining a flashlight on the steps. As we walked in the surroundings began to look familiar. Then we got up to the second floor and that same dark nasty energy was still there from the year before. I began to feel a little uncomfortable. The group was led into a large room with lots of windows. This large space was filled with glowing light of the moon. It had a heavy feeling to it. I think it was used for operations.

Then we moved into another space much larger than the operating room. I walked around for a little while and took digital photos and turned on my EVP recorder. Then I found myself standing in the middle of the room. Then I began to feel like I was the only one in the room. Something was getting ready to happen and I knew it. This next experience was overwhelming and very much unexpected.

My eyes were closed, and I noticed I was going into a channeling state. I was not able to stop it. Something or someone wanted to communicate with me at this exact moment. Then I felt a presence of a male spirit and he showed himself to me. He looked very skinny and extremely pale looking. His hair was short with a thin mustache. This man was still in his death state. I picked up on the word "Military". Then I heard him tell me he became terribly ill while serving in the military. I saw his facial bones and his arms and legs were also very bony. Suddenly he jumped into my body, which he did not do very well. I believe he jumped me to feel a physical body again. He missed the experience of physical life. I told him he had to get out of my body and when he did, he was gone. This occurrence probably took about five minutes when it seemed longer. I opened my eyes and noticed the other people around me. The aftermath was I became sick and exhausted. I was barely able to make it through the last two buildings. Feeling fatigued was becoming a problem and I told one of the guides I had to leave. Once I left the property, I started to feel a little better, but did not function until the next morning. It took two to three days to recover from the experience.

I do see myself returning to the old winery and I will be better prepared.

It is an amazing place to visit.

Conclusion

The spiritual journey in this book now comes to an end, but I believe my experiences will continue. Looking back through all occurrences, it has increased my faith in the spirit world. I genuinely believe we are not alone on this earth and spirits are everywhere. We may not always sense them, but they are here. I believe our ancestors are watching out for us. My grandmother, Mary Liz, still communicates with me from the other side. As a child, spirits were continuously communicating with me. It used to scare the daylights out of me. Looking back at it as an adult, I see it was my psychic abilities at work. I just had no idea that was the situation. I have also come to believe that some sprits are in the physical dimension and some are in the spirit realm.

I have talked a lot about psychic abilities and Reiki energy healing work. These two subjects do happen separately. Working with psychic abilities is communicating with the spirits or the dead bringing forth messages to family and friends. I look forward to helping more people by communicating with spirits in homes, businesses and personal readings and helping to clear out spirits who are causing disturbances with the living. Reiki applies healing energy to another living being by healing the soul and the physical body. I have studied Reiki in the hope of helping more people and animals with the healing. I believe healing is important during these times.

My belief in spirits became finalized when my dad's brother, Chuck, appeared long enough for me to see him with my physical eyes. This was the day after his death. Further evidence lay in the fact that I have been scratched, touched, heard footsteps, and have seen shadow figures.

Writing this book has inspired me to continue developing my psychic abilities. It is my belief we all have some level of psychic sensibility. I hope this book has been inspiring to readers who are ready to investigate their own psychic development. Perhaps such pursuit can help us to have a wider view of the world.

Blessings.

About the Author

Devin Listrom lives in Kansas City Missouri. He was born in 1969 and graduated from Park Hill High School. Devin studied vocal music and opera at the UMKC Conservatory of Music. He has been fascinated with ghosts and communicating with spirits since childhood, after he discovered that he could see and speak with them. Devin became interested in metaphysical subjects during his teenage years and has made it a lifelong study.

Devin does paranormal investigations for homes and businesses in the greater Kansas City area. He communicates with spirits, then asks them to move on if requested by the homeowner.

Devin owns a business called Healing Spirit and he practices energy healing and body work. He is a trained Reiki Master Energy Healer. Devin also offers psychic readings for individuals. He is a dedicated vegan and supporter of animal rights.

Devin is currently working on a new book which is a series of essays on the old nature religions from pre-Christian times.

Publications by Un-X Media

The Color Therapy Wall Chart 1999
Rules for Goddesses by Margie Kay 2003
Gateway to the Dead: A Ghost Hunter's Field Guide
2013 by Margie Kay
Un-X News Magazine 2001-2015
Family Secrets 2017 by Jean Walker
Haunted Independence, Missouri 2017 by Margie Kay
The Kansas City UFO Flaps 2017 by Margie Kay
The Remote Viewing Workbook 2019 by Margie Kay
A Sonoma County Phenomenon 2020 by Margie Kay
The Fast Movers by Margie Kay, Bill Spicer, and
Wayne Lawrence 2020
Doorway to Spirit by Devin Listrom 2020
I Survived beyond and Back by Tracie Austin 2020

And coming soon:
The Master Dowser's Chart Book by Margie Kay 2021
THOR by Margie Kay 2021
Real Aliens - Real People by OPUS 2021
Missouri UFO Hot Spot by Missouri MUFON 2021
Psychics and Law Enforcement 2021

www.unxmedia.com

Email: editor@unxmedia.com
All books available at Amazon.com
and BarnesandNoble.com
Wholesale orders welcome.